BRUCE A. HILL:
PANCREATIC CANCER WARRIOR

BRUCE A. HILL:
PANCREATIC CANCER WARRIOR

Be Good. Work Hard. Help Others.

Linda Hill

BRUCE A. HILL: PANCREATIC CANCER WARRIOR
BE GOOD. WORK HARD. HELP OTHERS.

iUniverse books may be ordered through booksellers or by contacting:

iUniverse
1663 Liberty Drive
Bloomington, IN 47403
www.iuniverse.com
844-349-9409

Because of the dynamic nature of the Internet, any web addresses or links contained in this book may have changed since publication and may no longer be valid. The views expressed in this work are solely those of the author and do not necessarily reflect the views of the publisher, and the publisher hereby disclaims any responsibility for them.

Any people depicted in stock imagery provided by Getty Images are models, and such images are being used for illustrative purposes only.
Certain stock imagery © Getty Images.

ISBN: 978-1-6632-0328-1 (sc)
ISBN: 978-1-6632-0329-8 (e)

Print information available on the last page.

iUniverse rev. date: 07/23/2020

This book is dedicated to all of the pancreatic cancer warriors who were taken from us too soon and to all of the survivors who continue to battle the Beast! Never Ever Give Up!

Introduction

Throughout my husband's three year battle with pancreatic cancer, I kept a health journal on his progress. At the same time, I was keeping a health journal on my own struggles with renal cancer. After Bruce passed, I printed up the journal I kept on him and distributed copies to close family and friends. The primary feedback I received was that Bruce's journal should reach a wider audience. Bruce was positive and optimistic throughout his three years as a cancer survivor and warrior. The one word used most to describe him throughout this period was "inspiration." It is my hope that by telling Bruce's story, he can, through the way he lived his life and ultimately, the way he faced death, continue to inspire, encourage, and give hope to those who may need it the most. As my friends in the Pancreatic Cancer NEGU group would say: NEVER EVER GIVE UP!

(NOTE: I have given the doctors, physician assistants, and nurses fictitious first names.)

 PART ONE

2015: October through December

Wednesday, 10/14:

Happy Anniversary to Bruce and me–#26! It was nice to celebrate another year together—especially after the way this year began.

When Bruce and I met through mutual friends in 1987, I was divorced with three young sons. Bruce had never been married. I made it clear from the outset that I wasn't interested in marriage so Bruce agreed to just be friends. He was wonderful to me and to my sons. My parents adored him! One day he drove me to Philadelphia to visit a friend who had multiple sclerosis and lived in a rehabilitation center. We decided to take Claudia out to lunch. That meant Bruce had to carry her into the car, put her wheelchair in the car, and wheel her into the restaurant. To my awe, I watched as Bruce gently fed Claudia—someone I'd known for years and whom he had just met. That was the day I remember looking at Bruce as more than just a friend. Over the following year, our friendship progressed to love and talks of marriage began. Since I was still reluctant to enter into another marriage, I brought Bruce to a family therapist I knew. He spoke with us together and then privately with Bruce. Afterwards, Bruce waited outside while the therapist talked briefly to me. He really only had one thing to say when I asked him to tell me what he thought of Bruce. He looked at me and said: "I think he's a diamond in the ruff." I valued his opinion and knew then and there that I was going to marry this "diamond in the ruff." On October 14, 1989, we were married at a little church in Hopatcong, New Jersey, with my sons taking part and our family, friends, and my first grade students present. Afterwards, we had a reception at the Chester Fire House. Bruce had been a volunteer fireman so the fire house was the perfect venue for us! It was a beautiful day for us and our families!

The next twenty-five years were typical of any couple with three growing sons. Bruce took a special interest in the boys and our lives were happy and content, though not without the usual problems of any married couple and parents. That is until November, 2014, when I had a routine blood test that indicated an abnormality. After several tests, I was diagnosed with a large mass on my left kidney. In January, 2015, I had the ten centimeter mass and my entire kidney removed. The mass was determined to be malignant. I heard the words, "renal cancer," for the first time. Thankfully, my surgeon was able to remove all of the cancer. My follow-up treatments would only be having Cat scans every three months. Eventually, I recovered from the surgery, adjusted to my "new normal," and life resumed—along with a lot of gratitude for my health as well as for Bruce, who was there for me every step of the way. That's why our twenty-sixth wedding anniversary today means even more to us than the previous twenty-five!

Saturday, 10/31:

Oh what a night! Bruce was in constant pain on the left side of his body yesterday and last night. I'd asked if he wanted to go to the E.R. but he didn't. He's never sick except for colds and sore throats so this was definitely out of character for him and it scared me. Aside from the fact that he's such a good, kind person and I don't want anything to happen to him, I also don't know what I'd do without him.

We went to Urgent Care this morning. The doctor said that at best, Bruce has acid reflux and at worse, he could have an ulcer or a hernia (Even those are better than what I was afraid of.). He gave Bruce a prescription for Nexium and had us go for blood work to see if it was stomach related. I'm grateful that what's wrong with Bruce doesn't appear to be anything serious.

Monday, 11/2:

Bruce and I went to his appointment with our gastro doctor, Dr. Jay. He's pretty certain that Bruce has an ulcer. Bruce will have an endoscopy and we'll know for certain then what's causing his pain.

Tuesday, 11/17:

Bruce and I had to be at the medical center at 7:15 a.m. His endoscopy was scheduled for 8:00 a.m. but didn't get underway til after 9:00. Dr. Jay said that Bruce had an ulcer years ago that has healed over his stomach. Bruce was unaware of having had an ulcer so I'm very confused by this. The doctor wants to do a Cat scan of the stomach and pelvis next. This is how I got started with everything last November so I'm very nervous about it. I expected to only hear that Bruce had an ulcer and that it would then be treated. I didn't expect to hear that he has to have a Cat scan. Also, Dr. Jay removed a small nodule which will be biopsied. He said it's "nothing to worry about." But I am worried. I can't believe Bruce and I are having serious health issues at the same time, just a year apart.

Wednesday, 11/18:

Bruce is in a lot of pain, especially at night. I'm so afraid this is something serious. I always assumed Bruce would live a long, healthy life because he takes such good care of himself. He thanked me for making all of the calls to get the insurance straightened out. That's the least I could do after all he's done and still does for me!

Tuesday, 11/24:

Bruce had a colonoscopy this morning. Thankfully, everything went well! The doctor only removed one polyp.

This evening, we went to a healing Mass at a church in Netcong. I pray that this special mass and the special blessing will manifest itself in the healing of my body and Bruce's.

Tuesday, 12/8:

Bruce had his first Cat scan this morning. The scan seems to show a tipped appendix that may require surgery. The confusing part is that Bruce's pain is entirely on his left side, not his right side, where the appendix is. I'm just so grateful that Bruce doesn't have cancer (Yes, my mind went there.)!

Wednesday, 12/9:

Bruce and I went to his appointment with our gastro doctor. Bruce's appendix is enlarged and needs to come out. The doctor thinks the pain Bruce has on his left side is back pain but Bruce doesn't think so. He knows back pain and he said that's not what this is.

Friday, 12/11:

Today we had Bruce's appointment with Dr. Steve, a surgical oncologist. After an exam and consult in his office, where he showed us Bruce's Cat scan and explained it, we got very scary and unexpected news: Although Bruce's appendix is enlarged and should be removed, it's not a danger and is a "secondary problem." Long story short: a duct from Bruce's pancreas is enlarged. I told the doctor he was scaring me. He said not to worry yet; it's probably a benign cyst, which is common. I don't like words like "yet" and "probably." Dr. Steve wants new scans and more blood work. Bruce and I left his office in disbelief and completely drained.

Saturday, 12/12:

Throughout my health ordeal from last November through last week, I never went on the internet with my symptoms. But I went on this morning to read about pancreatic cancer and now I'm beside myself! One of the signs is the exact type of pain Bruce has been having for a couple of months—pain from his stomach and left side of his chest around to the left side of his back. I'm beyond scared. I decided not to tell this to Bruce. I'll just hope and pray he doesn't have cancer and what the doctor said turns out to be correct—that it's a benign cyst.

Monday, 12/14:

Bruce and I did a little shopping this morning but had to cut our outing short as Bruce was in so much pain. After we got home, he took a nap, which he never does during the day. I'm so worried about him and am praying hard that he'll be alright.

Tuesday, 12/15:

Bruce slept on the living room floor last night. He was in terrible pain and couldn't get comfortable in bed. Thankfully, he was fine this morning. He even went to the gym and then to the movies. After he got home, he went back out for an Italian hotdog! I'm so nervous I can hardly eat and he's eating an Italian hotdog! Nothing stops him!

Wednesday, 12/16:

Bruce had a rare good night's sleep last night—he slept in our bed and without pain. He called it a miracle! He even felt well enough to go to Jake's school's holiday concert—a welcome distraction from what's been going on here.

Thursday, 12/17:

Bruce and I were at the hospital for about an hour and a half today. He had to have new Cat scans done. We won't know the results till tomorrow. I'm so nervous!

Friday, 12/18:

We had our appointment with surgical oncologist, Dr. Steve, today. He showed us yesterday's scans, which are clearer than the first set but show the same thing—an enlarged pancreatic duct. Bruce has to go for a special endoscopic ultrasound to see what's inside this duct. God forbid it's cancerous. If it isn't cancer we should still be able to go to Disney with Chris, Jen, and the kids. But if Bruce needs chemo, that pushes the surgery back and we won't be able to go. In that case, Bruce and I will both be heartbroken. My mind is spinning right now. We left this doctor and headed to our gastro doctor, Dr. Jay. He scheduled the ultrasound for Monday. They will take fluid out of the gland and biopsy it. We'll get the results in a couple of days. So next week will be crucial.

Saturday, 12/19:

I didn't sleep last night. Everything kept rolling around in my mind. I'm so worried about Bruce. I can't believe we're going through another health crisis and at the same time as mine last year. I'm praying so hard that Bruce will be okay.

Monday, 12/21:

Bruce and I went to the hospital for his endoscopy and an endoscopic ultrasound. We were told it would take a few days for the results of the biopsy but Dr. Jay told us right after the procedure that it was cancerous. We are shocked and devastated. Bruce will need eight weeks of chemo and then surgery. He said the tumor is small, isolated, and in its early stage.

He thinks Bruce will be okay. I certainly hope so. Bruce is optimistic and has an amazing attitude. I'm beyond scared and heartbroken. God only knows what our future holds now.

Tuesday, 12/22:

Dr. Steve called and explained everything to me. He thinks Bruce can beat this because the tumor is isolated and easy to remove. Also, there are no visible cancer cells in the liver or any lymph glands. He said Bruce will need eight weeks of chemo, surgery, and probably more chemo after that.

Bruce has been amazing—he was out the door at 5:30 a.m. to go to the gym and a few other places. He's still smiling and still carrying on—in complete faith that he will beat this terrible cancer. He is honestly handling this better than I am.

Wednesday, 12/23:

Bruce did a little shopping this afternoon and came home in a lot of pain and with a headache. He took a nap and then got up at dinnertime and ate a little. He was still in a lot of pain. I was SO worried about him. As scary as all of this is, Bruce continues to maintain a peaceful and positive attitude.

Maureen called and offered to take us to the hospital tomorrow even though we have to leave at 6:15 a.m. to have a port implanted for chemo. If Bruce weren't in so much pain I would've declined Maureen's offer. But I accepted her kindness. God bless her.

Thursday, 12/24:

WHAT A DAY! Bruce was in a lot of pain during the night so neither of us got much sleep. Thank God Maureen picked us up to go to the hospital. We got there by 7:00 a.m., registered, and went to same-day surgery. Maureen stayed with me the entire time. After the procedure, Dr. Steve came out and said it went well and that Bruce was in his room but not fully awake. I asked about the pain Bruce was in yesterday. The doctor said it's the tumor pressing against a nerve. He prescribed a stronger pain medication. Later, he came back and said he'd called Dr. Al, an oncologist, and asked if he could take Bruce today. I didn't want to bother Maureen again but she said she would take us there. When Bruce was fully awake, we went into his room. He was sitting up in bed and looked so much better than he did earlier. Dr. Steve came in to explain everything about the implant. He said he thinks Bruce has a really good chance of beating this. God, I hope so! After Bruce was released, Maureen drove us to our appointment with Dr. Al. As for the appointment, Bruce and I both loved the doctor! He was wonderful! We were with him for a while and he went over everything. He said Bruce is "lucky" that this was found early. He thinks the chemo and surgery will help Bruce. He said Bruce should not get sick from the chemo but if he does, they have treatments for it. The doctor said Bruce will mainly be tired after the chemo treatments. As for Disney, he said we can go and that he'll work around it. Bruce and I are thrilled! (I texted Chris and Jen and said: "Disney, here we come!") We got home around 2:00 p.m. Maureen came in for a few minutes. Carol told her she's an angel and asked where her wings were! I've said it before and I'll say it again: God bless Maureen!

Bruce went right to bed after we got home. He had wanted to come over to Chris and Jen's for Christmas Eve dinner but he couldn't. He was tired, had a headache, and was sore from the procedure. He was also feeling the effects of the anesthesia. I hated to leave him but I also didn't want to disappoint Chris, Jen, and the kids. Bruce and I were planning on telling the kids about Disney together but sadly, I had to do it without him. My heart wasn't in it but the kids were naturally thrilled! Chris videotaped their reactions so he could show it to Bruce at a later date.

Friday, 12/25:

Merry Christmas!

Bruce slept well last night and felt fine this morning. Maureen and Henry picked me up for church; I wouldn't let Bruce go. We made it over to Debbie's for dinner but Bruce didn't eat much. He became very tired so we left early.

Monday, 12/28:

I emailed the Pancreatic Cancer Action Network and got a long and detailed email back with lots of information. Bruce and I appreciated all of the info, especially since we know so little about this disease.

Bruce had a terrible night last night. He slept on the living room floor for a few hours. Tonight he begins his stronger meds. I hope they help him with his pain and that he'll then be able to sleep better. It's heartbreaking to see him like this.

Tuesday, 12/29:

Bruce slept better last night; the stronger pain meds are helping.

I called the head nurse at the Cancer Center. The chemo pills have been approved; the Pet scan hasn't. If Bruce has the Pet scan before Sunday, he can start chemo next Wednesday. We will have a 45 minute counseling session prior to chemo.

Bruce and I went to a healing Mass this evening. Last month it was for me; this time it was for Bruce.

Thursday, 12/31:

Happy New Year's Eve! I'm really glad 2015 is coming to an end.

I spent a lot of time on the phone with my insurance company, the hospital, and Dr. Al's office. My insurance won't cover the Pet scan for Bruce so the doctor ordered a bone scan and a chest scan (I had those prior to my surgery for the same reason.). Dr. Al said Bruce should start the chemo pills on Sunday. The scans are scheduled for Tuesday and the consult and chemo treatments are scheduled for Wednesday. We're on our way. I'm praying for a good outcome!

PART TWO

2016: January through December

Friday, 1/1:

Happy New Year! I pray Bruce gets through his health issues and that this will indeed be a happy year for both of us!

Tuesday, 1/5:

Bruce and I were at the hospital from around 7:30-11:15 this morning. He had a chest scan and a bone scan. After we got home and had lunch, Bruce went to the gym. God bless him!

Wednesday, 1/6:

Today was a day of total frustration! Bruce and I went to the Cancer Center for what was supposed to be his first chemo treatment. To begin with, it was surreal sitting in the sadly crowded waiting room and then being in the treatment room. I couldn't help wondering about the individual stories behind all those patients. When it was our turn, the nurse said that Bruce's port was infected and that they couldn't do the treatment. A few nurses came in and they all agreed chemo had to be postponed. They gave us a prescription for an antibiotic and sent us on our way. I had placed a call to Dr. Steve and he called back in the evening. He said it's hard to say what caused the infection as this is common with ports. He said the port had to come out and told us to meet him at the hospital tomorrow at 7:00 a.m. He'll remove the port and put a new one in the beginning of next week so that Bruce can have chemo next Wednesday. As for Bruce, his optimism and totally positive attitude about everything (even this) is unbelievable! He really is my hero!

Thursday, 1/7:

This was another incredulous day! Bruce and I arrived at the hospital around 6:30 a.m. By 7:00, Dr. Steve came into the room and shocked us with yet another turn of events. He spoke with Dr. Al last night and they both agreed that even if Bruce's port infection is minor, it would delay chemo and surgery. Both doctors think it's best to operate first and do chemo later. It threw us for a loop but naturally we agreed. So surgery will be this coming Monday! Then Bruce went into the operating room to have the port removed and a couple of stitches put in. I went into the waiting room—alone and feeling very weepy. I texted the family with the news. I texted Maureen and asked if she was up. She said yes so I called her. I just needed to talk to someone. She told me as soon as she'd read my text she knew it "wasn't good." Maureen said she'll help any way she can. This morning she helped just by listening to me.

Saturday, 1/9:

Mary, from Dr. Steve's office, called. Bruce is on the schedule for surgery for 1:00 p.m. on Monday, 1/11. I'm SO nervous!

Sunday, 1/10:

Bruce drove me over to Chris and Jen's and went in to see the kids. Jen told me later that Jake asked what was wrong with Papa Bruce and that she told him the truth. She's dreading telling Sean because he's such a worrier.

I was at Chris and Jen's for Jake's birthday party. I wouldn't let Bruce stay for it because I didn't want him exposed to so many people since his surgery is tomorrow. Doug drove me home so he could spend time with Bruce. After he left, Ann, David, and Carolina came to see Bruce. Carolina gave him rosary beads blessed by Pope Benjamin. I'm so grateful for all of the love, support, and prayers that Bruce and I are getting.

Monday, 1/11:

This was the longest, most nerve-wracking day of my life! Maureen dropped Bruce and me off at the hospital around 11:00 a.m. and I didn't get home til after 11:00 p.m. The day itself was surreal. They took Bruce into the O.R. around 12:30. I talked with Dr. Steve at 1:00. The surgery started shortly after that. It didn't end til around 10:00 p.m. Wayne and May were there from around noon to 7:00 p.m. Doug came after school and stayed til 8:30 p.m., when I told him he should go home. Debbie and Gianna were there from around 4:30 on. They drove me home and stayed overnight. There's no way I could go into all of the details so I'll have to summarize things. The cancer was more invasive than the scans showed. They removed the pancreatic duct, 70% of the pancreas, a small portion of the small intestine, and two infected veins. They removed Bruce's gall bladder as he had gall stones; they removed his appendix because it was enlarged; and they removed his spleen because it shares the same blood supply as the pancreas. The longest part of the surgery was the vascular part and waiting for each section they removed to be tested in pathology. That's how they knew how much to keep removing. Bruce didn't need any blood throughout the surgery and his vitals were fine throughout it. The nurses said the fact that Bruce is strong and in good shape definitely worked to his advantage. Throughout the surgery, a nurse would give us occasional updates but mostly we just sat there talking, staring at the clock, and waiting for news. It was agonizing! Debbie, May, and I kept the family informed through texts. Dr. Steve finally came in to talk to us around 10:30. He said he didn't leave any cancer in Bruce's body but everything now depends on the biopsy of the 23 lymph nodes. Regardless of what the biopsy shows, Bruce will need three to six months of chemo. It's going to be a very long haul. I just pray he gets through this. I'm so grateful this day is over and I'm especially grateful for Bruce's two surgeons.

Tuesday, 1/12:

I only slept around three hours last night; I was too scared and nervous. Debbie called the hospital to check on Bruce in the morning. He hadn't slept much and was in a lot of pain.

Maureen, Jen, and Colin came over in the morning. After they left, Debbie, Gianna, and I went to the hospital. Bruce was in a lot of pain and any noise, lights, and machines bothered him. He looked good as his coloring was back. But he definitely was in no mood to talk. Because they removed most of the pancreas, Bruce's sugar is a little high. The doctor will monitor it and will give him meds if the level doesn't come down in a few days. The pancreas can regenerate in a couple of weeks which means Bruce wouldn't be a diabetic long-term. This has been an emotionally exhausting day! I can't believe how my life and Bruce's have changed.

Wednesday, 1/13:

So many people have called, texted, sent private Face Book posts, etc. Bruce is well liked by so many people! Jen went to the hospital this morning and kept me posted. She said they had Bruce in a chair for over two hours—quite an achievement. They moved him by the window, which he'd wanted. Maureen and Henry drove me to the hospital. Bruce looked good and was talking more. But he was doing a lot of complaining, which is unlike him. The doctor told me that morpheme does that to people so he took Bruce off of it and put him on something less strong. A nun came in to see Bruce. I told her we were from St. Jude's and she came back later with a prayer shawl made by the ladies of St. Jude's. I asked for Father Paul, who's chaplain at the hospital and has served Masses at St. Jude's. He came right in and said the healing prayer for Bruce. Bruce was pretty funny with everyone there and we all had some well needed laughs! The case worker came in to see Bruce and talk with me. We can't plan for anything until we know when Bruce will be home. Dr. Steve came in and said that everything's "going as well as can be expected." He said we'll have the preliminary results of the biopsy tomorrow. That will be another anxious day.

Thursday, 1/14:

Maureen picked me up and drove me to the hospital. We got there around 12:30. Bruce was sitting in the chair and looked even better than yesterday. But he was hurting and asked to go back to bed. He had already been in the chair for over two hours so the nurse put him in bed at that point. While Maureen was there, Bruce began to cry. He said he was afraid of what the doctor was going to say. It was heartbreaking. After Maureen left, Bruce told me that he cried because he doesn't "want to leave" me and the "the boys." It was so sad. The nun came in and talked with me in the hall. She said crying is normal; this is a grieving process and it's good for Bruce to get it out. Dr. Steve said Bruce is doing well, his vitals are still good, and his sugar was fine today so he didn't need insulin. That means Bruce's pancreas has already begun to regenerate. The best news was that the preliminary biopsy on the nodes is negative! What a relief! However, the final biopsy, which will be much more detailed, won't be in until Monday. But we had great news tonight and I happily texted it to the family! Thank you, God!

Friday, 1/15:

Bruce looked good today! They had removed the catheter. His sugar is fine so no insulin. The noise and lights don't bother him as much as they did. The pain is manageable. His incision is very sore. It's hard to get comfortable in bed and that's his major complaint. The physical therapist came while I was there and got Bruce out of bed and walking with a walker down to the next room. It was a huge accomplishment! She also showed Bruce several exercises he can do in bed which he had no trouble doing. Thankfully, Bruce has always been in good shape. An internist came in and said that everything is going well. Bruce's brother, Bill, called while everyone was there. I put my phone on speaker so he could talk to Bruce. Bill was great but Bruce became very emotional and began to cry so I had to get back on the phone. I think everything's just hitting him and I don't think he realized how many people love him.

Wayne and May visited today. Debbie, Chris, Jen, and the boys also visited. Jake went over to the side of Bruce's bed. He wanted to see where "the doctor cut Papa Bruce." In the parking lot, Jake asked me if Papa Bruce would be out of the hospital before Disney. Jen said he and Sean had already asked her that. I can't see how we're going to make Disney but we still have two more weeks to decide.

Chris drove me home and put the new t.v. stand that Bruce had bought together. Bruce wants Chris to buy a t.v. we saw at Sam's and hook it up before he comes home from the hospital. None of this is necessary but how do I say no to Bruce now?!

Saturday, 1/16:

Dr. Steve took the tube out of Bruce's nose last night. Bruce is walking with the walker unassisted now! Another accomplishment!

Sunday, 1/17:

Dr. Al came in today and gave me (And Doug, who thankfully was with me.) very discouraging news. He said even though they got all the cancer out and the preliminary biopsy was negative, this cancer has a high probability of coming back. After that he said it's "in God's hands." I was crushed. Thank God I had Doug to talk to. I texted the family to tell them. Debbie and May immediately called. I decided not to tell Bruce what Dr. Al said.

Bruce's cousin, Jeff, and his wife, Cherry, came to visit. I told them in the hall what Dr. Al had said. Cherry works in a nursing home and said that pancreatic cancer is the worst cancer. I'm so sad.

Monday, 1/18:

I didn't sleep well after talking with Dr. Al. But today, things started to look up! Today's Martin Luther King's birthday and the boys and Chris had off so Chris, Sean, and Jake picked me up this morning and brought me to the hospital. Dr. Steve walked in right after we did—and he had VERY GOOD news! The full pathology report came in and all 23 lymph nodes that Dr. Steve removed were negative! So was the piece of intestine that was removed. Dr. Steve thinks that with chemo, Bruce has a good shot at beating this terrible disease! I could've kissed Dr. Steve! I'm beyond grateful! I was so glad Chris was with me at the time. He and I immediately started texting the family to let them know. Thank you, God!!!

After Chris and the boys left, I was alone with Bruce all day. He will have a visiting nurse and a physical therapist at home for the time being. I'm very happy about that. I'm even happier that Bruce will be coming home tomorrow morning! I know we have a long road ahead but I can't wait to just have him home!

Tuesday, 1/19:

A momentous day!

I called the hospital to let them know what time we'd be there. Chris picked me up and we got to the hospital around 10:00 a.m. The endocrinologist was there. Because Bruce's sugar was slightly elevated, we have to check it at home. We got our discharge information after this doctor left the room. The nurse in charge said what a "good patient" Bruce was and that they're going to miss him.

We got home around noon. Bruce made it up the stairs unassisted but had to sit in the living room afterwards. Bruce ate very little today. He was in a lot of pain and the Percoset didn't help much. He also is having pain in his lower back, which he said is not from the surgery. He shaved and took a shower. Showering wasn't easy since he has that drainage port in his body. I helped him dry himself, especially his legs and feet, which he can't do by himself.

Wednesday, 1/20:

Today was my first calm day in a long time. Bruce, though in pain, seemed better. He's walking up and down the hallway with his walker. He drank an Instant Breakfast shake with a banana and berries in it. Later he ate a scrambled egg—the most he's had since prior to his surgery.

The visiting nurse came this morning. We really liked her and she was very helpful. She thinks Bruce is progressing nicely. She'll be back on Monday.

Thursday, 1/21:

My kidney surgery was one year today, which means I'm one year cancer free. Thank you, Jesus!

Wayne and May came up and stayed around two hours. Bruce sat with us in the living room the entire time! He even said he felt good the whole time. It was probably good for him to be out of bed that long. He's doing a lot of walking with his walker. The physical therapist called. She's going to come tomorrow afternoon if Bruce isn't too tired from going to the doctor.

Bruce mentioned going to Disney today. He goes up and down with this depending on how he feels. We're all hoping he'll make it. What an achievement that would be after all Bruce has been through!

Friday, 1/22:

Bruce walked down the stairs and outside by himself, just using the cane—he continues to amaze me! At our appointment, Dr. Steve removed all of Bruce's staples. He's keeping the port for the juices in till next week. He wants chemo to start right away. He said they're going to be very proactive with this and are "going to throw everything in but the kitchen sink" to help Bruce beat this. God willing, he will do just that! Dr. Steve said that Bruce's attitude and the fact that he was in such good shape helped him through the very long and arduous surgery.

Monday, 1/25:

Bruce was in a lot of pain today. I think everything has worn off and he's feeling the effects of surgery. He's eating minimally and still can't sleep. I feel so badly for him. A different nurse came today. We mostly talked about nutrition.

Bruce's surgery was two weeks today. I posted a picture of him walking with his cane in the driveway on Face Book and wrote a little something about him. I've gotten so many beautiful comments from it. Bruce seems to be inspiring a lot of people with his attitude!

Tuesday, 1/26:

The physical therapist came today. She said Bruce is doing well. Too bad she can't control his pain.

Maren, from the Pancreatic Cancer Network, called after getting my email about Bruce's pain and digestive problems. She was a big help and followed up all of the info she gave me over the phone in an email. I'm glad I reached out to her.

Thursday, 1/28:

Bruce's friend, Bob, picked us up at 6:20 a.m. and drove us to the hospital. Bruce had the chemo port put in and the port for the pancreatic juices removed. Dr. Steve wants Bruce to eat more and to drink Boost three times a day. He prescribed something for his stomach and stronger pain meds. It was terrible being alone in the waiting room all that time. I spent a lot of time just staring at the room opposite from where I waited over eight hours the day of Bruce's surgery.

Friday, 1/29:

The visiting nurse and physical therapist came today. The nurse was very pleased with everything. The physical therapist took Bruce for a walk. He used his cane and did very well!

Saturday, 1/30:

Douglas, Michael, Bruce, and I went over to Chris and Jen's for Chris' surprise 40th birthday party. Chris was surprised to see Bruce and gave him a big hug! Bruce ate well; he even had a small piece of cake. Everyone was happy to see him!

After we got home, Bruce went outside for a little walk by himself. He told me how much he loved being at Chris and Jen's, out of the house, and with other people. I'm so glad he made it there today!

Michael texted when he was on the train, on his way home from here. He said how good it was to see Bruce and how "amazing" Bruce is. I'm so happy that the boys and everyone else are seeing this side of Bruce. He truly is an inspiration to all of us!

Sunday, 1/31:

Bruce wanted to go to church this morning so he did—the first time in three weeks. He had to sit throughout Mass but he made it! After we got home, he went for a walk. He's eating real food in small amounts. We're making progress!

Monday, 2/1:

Bruce had a very bad day—he was in pain all day. I felt so sorry for him. I'm sure it's surgical but it's scary whenever he's in pain. I can't help thinking dark thoughts.

Today was a very sad day for other reasons. Bruce and I brought Puffy to the Vet to be put down. She was fourteen and had lots of problems. The Vet said her organs were beginning to shut down. Hopefully, Puffy will be reunited with Mom and Dad. RIP, Puffy!

Tuesday, 2/2:

The physical therapist and two nursing students came today. Bruce's vitals are good. I wish Bruce would start eating. He only eats very small portions as he gets cramps when he eats. Even with medication, he's struggling. Bruce took three walks today, about ten minutes each. I went with him twice and the P/T took him out when she was here.

Wednesday, 2/3:

Today we went to Tommy's house and he drove us to our doctor appointment. Dr. Al said that Bruce looked "great." He was very pleased with how the surgery went and that the biopsy was completely clear. He said the surgery Dr. Steve did is normally only done in larger hospitals. He said most patients who undergo this type of surgery don't do nearly as well as Bruce did. Because pancreatic cancer is so bad, Bruce will have three months of chemo and then radiation. We already made the appointment with the doctor who will do the radiation as he's in the same building as Dr. Al. It's fine for us to go to Disney as that will be an "off week" from chemo. Chemo will begin the week after next.

Thursday, 2/4:

Wayne and May visited today. They were here while the visiting nurse came. Bruce's vitals were all good.

Friday, 2/5:

J.P. picked us up this morning to take me to a doctor appointment in Livingston. Bruce came because he said he just had "to get out of the house." He and J.P. went to the cafeteria while I was with the doctor.

Saturday, 2/6:

Bruce started on a pancreatic enzyme supplement today. Dr. Steve doesn't want him to lose any more weight. Bruce and I went to a furniture store to buy him a new recliner. He used his cane to get around the store. He'd been desiring a sandwich so we went to Subway. Bruce only ate two bites and had to stop as he felt full.

Sunday, 2/7:

Bruce drove to Shop Rite today for the first time since his surgery (I went with him.). Later, we went to the high school track and walked a mile—the furthest Bruce has gone at one time in a while. After we got home, he took a nap for a couple of hours. The walk might have been too much for him but he said he really enjoyed it!

Monday, 2/8:

Today we had an appointment with Bruce's surgeon. Dr. Steve is pleased with Bruce's progress. He remarked on how he "took a lot" out of Bruce. We don't go back to Dr. Steve for another two months.

Tuesday, 2/9:

Donna, the P/T, and two nurses came today. Donna had Bruce on the treadmill for ten minutes. He did very well!

BIG step for Bruce: He drove to Rockaway and went to the movies this afternoon by himself! He came straight home, said he did well, but that his back was hurting. I'm sure it was from sitting for so long. Regardless, Bruce loved doing something independently for the first time since before his surgery.

Wednesday, 2/10:

Bruce was in a lot of pain all day and nothing helped. Even though he said sitting in the chair at the movie theatre felt good, I can't help thinking that sitting that long without moving around aggravated his back.

Thursday, 2/11:

Today we met with Dr. Carl, who will do Bruce's radiation. He explained how the radiation will work. Regarding nutrition, he said to avoid sugar and fat. The one disturbing thing he said was what Dr. Al told Doug and me in the hospital—that pancreatic cancer has a high probability of returning. That's why they do both chemo and radiation. You can't get at every lymph gland in surgery so chemo is also to kill any possible remaining microscopic cancer cells.

Unfortunately, Bruce's pain got progressively worse throughout the day and nothing helped. I'm so worried about him.

Friday, 2/12:

Bruce continues to be in severe pain and it seems to be getting worse. It's still on his left side and back. I want so much to help him and there's nothing I can do. I keep praying for his pain to be relieved and will continue to do so. I called the Cancer Center and explained everything to the P.A. She said I can give Bruce two pain pills and he can take them every three hours, rather than every four.

Saturday, 2/13:

Bruce was in a lot of pain when he woke up—still on his left side and back. I started him on the pain meds every three hours, as the P.A. suggested. It did seem to give him some relief. He was able to sit out on the porch and watch t.v. most of the day. Also, he stayed up till a little after 8:00 p.m.—he's been going to bed around 7:00/7:30 since all of this started. It's so sad seeing him like this and oh, so scary.

Sunday, 2/14:

Bruce told me that this was the first Valentine's Day he'd "forgotten" to get me anything. I told him he didn't forget; he was incapacitated.

Monday, 2/15:

This morning, Bruce and I went shopping so he could buy shorts and a bathing suit for Florida. I could tell he was in pain and it went downhill after that. He was in terrible pain all day and spent most of the rest of the day in bed. The pain is where it's always been—on his left side. He's miserable and I can't help him.

Tuesday, 2/16:

Bruce had his first chemo treatment today. Chemo lasted two hours, not counting waiting, blood work, and consulting with the P.A. It's very depressing seeing all those people, all ages, and all of whom have cancer. I can't even describe my feelings. I just sat there with Bruce during his chemo. Bruce did well and the time went faster than I'd expected. Round one is now over. Bruce was in a lot of pain by the time we got home.

Wednesday, 2/17:

The P/T came for the last time. We're really going to miss her. Despite his pain, she thinks Bruce is doing well. In the afternoon, Bruce was light-headed. I hated having to leave him but I had to go to the drugstore to pick up his meds.

Thursday, 2/18:

Bruce had a very good day, thank God! His pain subsided, he looked good, he went for a half hour walk, he didn't take any naps, and he stayed up til 8:30, the latest he's been up in a month. I'm praying this continues.

Friday, 2/19:

Well, yesterday might have been a good day for Bruce but today definitely wasn't. He had a headache most of the day and felt nauseous throughout the day, despite eating very little.

Saturday, 2/20:

Debbie and family came up today. Debbie made soup for Bruce. Bruce was very quiet all day but was pretty good otherwise. As for me, I loved having company! It was so nice to have people to talk to and laugh with!

Sunday, 2/21:

Bruce was in a lot of pain all day. His new pain medication makes him light-headed. We really need to find out what's causing this pain; it's gone on way too long!

Monday, 2/22:

Bruce had a very bad night as he was in terrible pain. He slept downstairs but when he came up at 2:00 a.m. for a pain pill and complaining about his pain, I went into overdrive and never went back to sleep. I decided we can't go to Disney so I unpacked our suitcases. I texted Chris to tell him. When Debbie called, I just broke down and cried. It's just all too much. Right before Bruce's surgery, my doctor gave me a prescription for Xanax. I didn't take it then but I took it today.

Tuesday, 2/23:

Bruce slept well and felt so good this morning that now he wants to go to Disney! And I had completely unpacked! Here we go again.

Bruce and I went to his second chemo treatment this afternoon. I got the note I needed to get Bruce's meds through the airport. He has to go down tomorrow for a blood infusion to prevent infections. We talked with Dr. Al about Bruce's pain on his side and back. He doesn't think it's cancer related.

Wednesday, 2/24:

Bruce felt good all day! He went to the bank, post office, and drug store by himself for the first time in about six weeks! He also went to the Cancer Center by himself. Bruce got a blood infusion there.

Saturday, 2/27:

We left for Chris and Jen's at 4:30 a.m. Then it was off to Newark Airport and on to Florida! We had a very smooth flight. Chris had arranged for a wheelchair for Bruce at both airports. After we landed and got to our hotel, Bruce was tired so we went to our room and got settled. The kids went to Magic Kingdom. Bruce apologized to me for sometimes being "grumpy." He also thanked me for all I do for him. It was very sweet.

Monday, 2/29:

Bruce wasn't good today—he was very depressed and sad. He said he thinks about his brother Bob, who died from colon cancer, and wonders if he's going to end up the same way. It was heartbreaking.

Tuesday, 3/1:

Bruce is mostly staying in our hotel suite; even for meals. Today I went to the Magic Kingdom with the kids and didn't get back til 6:30. So Bruce was alone all day. I called several times to check on him. As much as I enjoyed being with the kids, I was not at ease since I was worried about Bruce all day. Turns out he was fine—he said he went for walks, sat by the pool, and rested in the room.

Wednesday, 3/2:

Bruce and I went to Animal Kingdom with the kids—Bruce's first venture to one of the parks! Chris pushed him in a wheelchair. Bruce only lasted half a day but he loved it! We were all so glad he was able to join us today. Bruce and I went back to the hotel, got lunch, and ate in our room. Bruce was tired and in pain, and didn't eat much. But of course, he said it was worth it to be with the family at Animal Kingdom!

Thursday, 3/3:

Bruce and I went for a long walk this morning. The weather's been beautiful and it's a very peaceful place to walk around. Bill drove up to see Bruce. Bruce felt better and loved spending time with his brother! We even ate dinner together in the food court. Bruce ate well; I'm sure seeing Bill was very good medicine for him!

Friday, 3/4:

Bruce had a bad night; he has the most pain at night, in his back. When he felt better, we went for a long walk and sat by the pool. It was very peaceful. As they say, water is very soothing.

Saturday, 3/5:

We headed home today. Bruce ate a sandwich and had a milkshake while we were waiting at the airport for our flight. It was the most he's eaten at one time in a while. Even Jake noticed it and said: "Papa Bruce must be getting better because he's eating again." It was a long week but I'm sure glad we made it! God bless Bruce—what a trooper he is!

Monday, 3/7:

Bruce took me for my Cat scans this morning. From Ambulatory Care we went to breakfast—first time for Bruce in over two months. He ate well and really enjoyed it!

Tuesday, 3/8:

Bruce had chemo this morning and did well! After we got home, we went back out to my appointment with Dr. Sam, my oncologist. He had read Bruce's reports, which I had forwarded to him. He said Dr. Al is very good and he agrees with Bruce's protocol. I was very happy to hear that.

After we got home, Bruce was fine til around 7:00 p.m. and then his stomach hurt so badly that he had to go to bed. He got up around 8:00, said his stomach felt better but that he was sweating so badly he had to change his tee shirt. I'm sure it's the chemo.

Wednesday, 3/9:

Bruce said he had the sweats during the night and had to change his shirt again. After breakfast, his stomach began to hurt. But as the day progressed, he began to feel better. In fact, today ended up being Bruce's best day since before his surgery! He felt good, ate well, went to recycling, and blew the leaves outside. It was sunny and in the 70s and Bruce really enjoyed being outside. He even went back out later on. It was great to see him doing something "normal" and feeling so well!

Thursday, 3/10:

Bruce had a very good day! He went to the deli to meet up with his friends, he went to the store, and he worked on the lawn. It was great to see him enjoying being outside on an unusually warm day. However, he was very tired in the afternoon and took a three hour nap. He felt great after he woke up!

Friday, 3/11:

Bruce and I went food shopping and he even came in with me—first time since before his surgery. Later, he went to the movies. I was worried the seats would hurt his back but he said he was fine. His pain started up after he ate something for dinner. He took his first pain pill of the day, walked around, and went to bed around 7:00 p.m. I think he has to learn to pace himself. But he's come a long way! From pain pills every three hours with no relief to one pill a day with relief! He's not even using the cane anymore! I'm praying his progress continues!

Monday, 3/14:

Bruce and I went to Mass this morning since it was being offered for him. It was weird but comforting to hear Bruce's name at the beginning of Mass.

Bruce took care of Piper today. He just had to let her out. He's not ready to walk her yet. From there, Bruce went for milk and to the post office. I think he likes doing these little chores by himself again.

Tuesday, 3/15:

Bruce had chemo this morning. He gained three pounds and his blood work and markers were all good! From the Cancer Center, we went out to lunch and then to the store. Bruce was very tired afterwards and took a nap. He also had stomach cramps after dinner. He felt better after walking around and then lying down for a while.

Thursday, 3/17:

Today Bruce took his car for service and was gone for a few hours. Later he went for a walk by himself. It might have been too much for him because he was tired and went to bed early.

Friday, 3/18:

This afternoon, Bruce and I went to Landing Park for a walk. Afterwards, he was very tired and went to bed early again.

Sunday, 3/20:

Bruce felt pretty good today so we met Doug for breakfast and went to the store afterwards. Later, Bruce went to bed at 6:15 and slept til 8:00. Then he got up and watched t.v. til around 11:00. He either naps during the day or goes to bed very early. He still has some pain and still has diarrhea. I feel so badly for him.

Tuesday, 3/22:

Bruce had his best day since his surgery: He looked good; he ate well; he worked outside for a while; he went to the post office by himself; he went to our accountant by himself; he didn't take a nap; and he stayed up till around 10:00 p.m. (His usual bedtime.). What a difference! I hope it lasts!

Thursday, 3/24:

Bruce and I went to his appointment with Dr. Al. Everything's fine. Bruce told Dr. Al that he's going "to be a new man" when this is all over. Dr. Al said: "God willing."

Saturday, 3/26:

Bruce and I went for a long walk today. He feels so much better when he's walking.

Sunday, 3/27:

Happy Easter! This holiday has special meaning to us after all Bruce has been through. Bruce enjoyed having the family here for dinner. He even ate a lot and had no problems. It was great watching him eat and enjoying it! He also sat with us the entire time. That alone made my day! It was probably the most relaxing day I've had since before Bruce's surgery.

Tuesday, 3/29:

Bruce and I went to chemo this morning. We had to go next door to make an appointment with Dr. Carl as radiation will be starting soon.

Saturday, 4/2:

Bruce had a great day! He felt well, he went to recycling, he went to buy some plants for out front, he did some planting, and he even went to church by himself. He never ceases to amaze me!

Sunday, 4/3:

Bruce went to the Mall to walk since it was too cold to walk outside. He's very committed to his walking regimen.

Monday, 4/4:

Bruce had a great day! He went to the movies, had lunch at the food court, walked around the Mall, and went to a few stores. He said he felt so good being out of the house and doing so much on his own. I'm so proud of him!

Tuesday, 4/5:

Bruce had his last "long" chemo today (God willing.). Next week he has off and after that, he'll have radiation plus a lighter dose of chemo for a shorter time. He got a massage while he was getting chemo.

Thursday, 4/7:

Bruce and I went to Shop Rite and when we got home, he had to sit on the step outside. He hadn't eaten breakfast and had gone for his walk before we went food shopping so he thinks he was just weak from all of the walking. A little while later, he fell asleep on the porch and then went to bed. He was in bed most of the afternoon. He said his stomach hurt. Every time something hurts him I can't help but think the worst. It's very, very scary.

Friday, 4/8:

Bruce felt much better today. This was his last day of chemo pills (Hopefully for good!). He saw a segment on the news about a stewardess who died from pancreatic cancer. He's been very depressed since seeing it. I missed it and Bruce won't talk about it. I believe the reality of what he's going through is starting to hit him. No one can expect him to be optimistic all of the time.

Tuesday, 4/12:

Bruce and I went to his appointment with Dr. Carl this morning. He thought Bruce looked good—much better than the first time he saw him. Radiation will be every weekday for 28 days. All of this is dependent on the Cat scan Dr. Carl ordered for Friday. The doctor said that while he's not expecting anything, if there were to be cancer cells, they would show up in Bruce's liver. In that case, he'd have to go back on strong chemo; radiation wouldn't help. Bruce is optimistic, as is Dr. Carl. As always, I'm nervous.

Thursday, 4/14:

Bruce and I went to his appointment with Dr. Al. He told Bruce that pancreatic cancer is the "worst cancer" and that it has a high rate of returning (He'd already told me this when Bruce was in the hospital but I never told Bruce.). Because of this, Bruce will need three more rounds of chemo after radiation is over. Of course, this is assuming tomorrow's Cat scan is clear. Bruce said later than knowing how bad his cancer is makes him want to fight even harder. He's truly amazing!

Friday, 4/15:

Another day of sitting, waiting and worrying. Bruce and I had to be at the hospital by 7:00 a.m. for his first post-op Cat scan. It took longer than I'd expected so I spent a lot of time sitting in the waiting room. We never heard from the doctor so I'm hoping that's a good sign. Unlike me, Bruce wasn't all that worried about it.

Saturday, 4/16:

Bruce fired up the grill for the first time this season and grilled hamburgers for dinner. We sat outside to eat—just the two of us. After dinner, we went to Mass. This may sound trivial but when you're dealing with cancer, any so called "normal" day is an absolute blessing!

Sunday, 4/17:

I got an email this morning regarding Bruce's Cat scan. While his liver is normal, the report mentioned a swelling at the tip of the pancreas that could indicate a "neoplasm." I looked that up and found out it means a tumor. The recommendation was for a Pet scan or another Cat scan. Of course, Bruce and I are very concerned about this.

Monday, 4/18:

Bruce and I took advantage of a beautiful day and went down to Long Branch. The day would've been perfect if Dr. Carl's associate hadn't called us on our way down. Unfortunately, I read Bruce's scan correctly. There's a swelling at the tip of his pancreas that could be nothing or could be another tumor. Now Bruce has to have a Pet scan and radiation is on hold. Bruce is as optimistic as ever. I'm very upset. He looks good, he feels good, and he's eating normally. How could something be wrong now?

Wednesday, 4/20:

Bruce and I got to the hospital for Bruce's Pet scan around 9:00 a.m. When Bruce came out around 11:30, the nurse said how "wonderful" Bruce is and how "lucky" I am. I'll consider myself lucky when we get good results from his scan!

Thursday, 4/21:

A very good day indeed! This morning, Dr. Carl called with very good news: Bruce's scan is fine; no cancer in his liver or anywhere else! Dr. Carl said when he looked at the Cat scan, he thought the swelling was from surgery and it was. He said the radiologist was being cautious by recommending a Pet scan. He did add that there were "probably" cancer cells in Bruce's body that aren't visible. That's why he's being treated aggressively. Dr. Carl asked if Bruce could be at the Cancer Center by 11:00 for the radiation simulation. Of course Bruce went right down. He spoke with the doctor, the head oncology nurse, and the radiologist who will be doing the treatments. Bruce got a lot of info about the whole process. He felt very good after talking with the doctor and the others. He came home relieved and anxious to talk to me about everything. I was so glad it worked out for him! The first treatment is next Wednesday.

Friday, 4/22:

Bruce felt good today so we went to the Crossings Outlets. We had lunch and did a little shopping. It was so nice to have a relaxing day after a stressful week.

Monday, 4/25:

Today Bruce went to the Nursery and bought flowers and a tree for out front, which he then planted. It was amazing to watch him digging with a shovel after all he's been through! He also went to the store to meet up with his friends. Later on he went to Lowe's and then came home and mowed the lawn. I just can't believe all he did today—just like "old times." Also, Bruce is walking up to two miles a day now!

Wednesday, 4/27:

Bruce and I went to the Cancer Center this afternoon. First we had to set up his chemo schedule. That starts next week. The chemo treatment room was packed. I hate this disease SO much! After that, we went next door to the radiation part. They showed me the room and explained everything to me. Bruce tolerated radiation very well! Later on, he was outside planting flowers. You'd never know what he'd been through!

Thursday, 4/28:

Bruce and I went to radiation #2. Bruce did well again. They did say that like chemo, radiation has a cumulative effect. Bruce might not have any aftereffects till around the midway point. After his treatment, we met with the oncology nutritionist. We were with her for a long time as she had a lot to tell us and we had a lot of questions.

Bruce and I went to a healing Mass at St. Jude's this evening. It was a long but beautiful service. I hope God answers my prayers and that tonight's healing helps both of us.

Friday, 4/29:

Bruce went to radiation by himself for the first time. He said it only took about ten minutes and that he was fine.

Saturday, 4/30:

After Mass, Bruce went over to talk to Father Tom. Father asked Bruce how life was treating him. Bruce said: "It could be better." Father Tom told Bruce that they should talk. I hope they do as I think it would be good for Bruce to talk to someone about what he's going through.

Monday, 5/2:

Bruce went to radiation by himself. So far so good! He looks fine, is eating well, and walks every day.

Tuesday, 5/3:

Bruce had radiation and chemo today. His blood work was good and he's gained ten pounds in a month! Way to go, Bruce!

Friday, 5/6:

Bruce and I went to radiation and then to Dr. Steve for a four months' check-up. He's pleased with Bruce's progress. He said the fact that the first post-op Pet scan was clear is a good sign. He told us how complicated Bruce's surgery was. Bruce told him how calm he felt going into surgery. I told Dr. Steve he should have put ME to sleep for ten hours! As always, we thanked him for all he's done for Bruce.

Saturday, 5/7:

Except for the weather, this was a great day! It was Dylan's annual Dinosaur Stomp. As usual, it rained—lightly but enough to make it cold and damp. What made this day so amazing was that Bruce did the 5K walk! He walked with Doug and Steve. Prior to the race, I asked them to stay with Bruce in case he needed them. But I should have known better than to doubt Bruce—he completed the very hilly 5K without any help from anyone—and less than four months post surgery! I was so proud of him! So many people were there to cheer him on. Maureen said she thought she was going to cry. I almost did. At the end of the day, I read beautiful and heartwarming comments on Face Book about Bruce's accomplishment today. He's inspired so many people, myself included.

Monday, 5/9:

When I was at radiation with Bruce, I showed the nurses and masseuse Bruce's pictures from the 5K he did. They were very impressed!

Wednesday, 5/11:

Bruce went to radiation and met with Dr. Carl who said everything's going well. Dr. Carl said he wishes all of his patients had Bruce's attitude!

Thursday, 5/12:

After radiation, Bruce and I went to my doctor as I needed blood work. From there, we met Doug at the Hilton in Rockaway to attend a program on spirituality. Bruce sat with a medium for a reading while I took notes. Among other things, the medium said that Archangel Jophiel, the archangel of healing, came through (The medium didn't know about our health issues.). She said that green is healing and that Bruce and I should picture ourselves in a green bubble every day and pray for healing. Archangel Orion, the angel of manifesting miracles, appeared. The medium said to pray for a miracle and not to rule one out. That was a nice way to end an interesting reading!

Sunday, 5/15:

Happy Birthday, Bruce–#63—and many, many more!!! Bruce and I met Doug in Denville and took the train into New York City. We walked to a place for breakfast and then walked to the harbor where we took the Circle Line. That was a two and a half hour ride. After that we went out to lunch and then walked around a street fair on our way back to Port Authority. It was a really nice day and a very special birthday for Bruce!

Tuesday, 5/24:

I went with Bruce to radiation #20 and to chemo. His blood work, vitals, and weight are all good. He really is amazing everyone, especially the medical professionals!

Wednesday, 5/25:

Another busy day in this new "journey" of ours. Bruce and I went to radiation #21. We met with Dr. Carl afterwards. He's very pleased with Bruce's progress, blood counts, and vital signs. He said that he doesn't expect Bruce to have any problems with the remainder of his radiation treatments. Another small miracle!

After radiation, we went to the Mall for lunch and then went back to the Cancer Center for the support group—the first one we were free to attend. The social worker said she thinks Bruce has a lot to offer these meetings (So do I.). She told us about the Race for Life programs and gave us a listing of them. One is a week from Saturday. I've already registered for it. The most encouraging thing the social worker said was that, thanks to improved surgeries and treatments for pancreatic cancer, more people are surviving it. After listening to her and to a woman whose brother had the Whipple eight years ago and is doing well, I finally feel cautiously optimistic that Bruce can beat this! From my lips to God's ears!

Friday, 5/27:

This has nothing to do with Bruce's health news but we got BIG news today while we were at Chris and Jen's! Jen's three and a half months pregnant and IT'S A GIRL!!! After three sons and five grandsons, we're finally going to have a baby girl in the family! Bruce and I are thrilled!

Tuesday, 5/31:

Bruce went to radiation #24 by himself this morning. It went very well. In the afternoon, he and I went to chemo together.

Wednesday, 6/1:

Bruce had radiation today and saw Dr. Carl's partner. The staff told Bruce they're going to miss him there (Radiation ends on Monday.). Everywhere Bruce goes he makes an impression and people miss him when he's not there. God bless him!

Saturday, 6/4:

This was a very sad day in the Hill family: Ann Hill passed away this morning after a brief battle with colon cancer—the same cancer that took Bob. It's heartbreaking.

Bruce and I went to our first Relay for Life sponsored by the American Cancer Society. We walked with the survivors and then we walked with the caregivers. Bruce and I are both survivors and caregivers. Finally, we walked for Dad, Bob, and Ann. It was very emotional. I posted a picture of our medals on Face Book and got a lot of nice comments back. Everyone seems to think Bruce and I are very "strong" and "courageous" when we're just living this crazy, scary life of ours.

Sunday, 6/5:

Bruce felt fine today so we went to Bianca's 24th birthday party. I was so glad he was well enough to attend the party! He even ate well!

Tuesday, 6/7:

Bruce and I went to his last radiation! We brought a tray of cookies and I wrote out a thank-you card for the doctor and staff. They were most appreciative. After Bruce's treatment, we met with the doctor. He said Bruce has done very well. We go back in three weeks. From there we went to the chemo room. Bruce's blood work and cancer markers continue to be fine. Dr. Al also said how well Bruce is doing. He said Bruce didn't need chemo today and won't have it for another two weeks. That will give his body a chance to rest after all the radiation. Then Bruce goes back on the strong chemo—three cycles; two weeks on and one week off. That should take us to the beginning of August. God willing, that will be it!

Wednesday, 6/8:

Bruce and I went to Colin's program at school. We try to go to as many of the boys' sports' events and school programs as possible. It helps us to feel "normal," and hopefully helps the kids to see that we're okay.

Friday, 6/10:

Today we went to Sean's class program on people who have contributed to society. Sean chose Steve Jobs since he died from pancreatic cancer. Sean was dressed like Jobs and did an excellent job explaining Jobs' background, including his diagnosis of and eventual death from pancreatic cancer. Bruce and I were so moved that Sean would choose Steve Jobs and so very proud of how well he portrayed him today.

Saturday, 6/11:

Bruce took me for my Cat scans early this morning. I don't know what I would do without him and I truly hope I never have to find out.

Sunday, 6/12:

Bruce and I went to Maureen's 70th birthday party at St. Jude's. Several people came over to ask Bruce how he was doing. They all said how good he looked. A couple said that Bruce was an "inspiration." That's the word we hear most often to describe Bruce and it's totally appropriate.

Tuesday, 6/14:

Bruce and I went to my appointment with Dr. Sam. I still have that nodule on my right lung but Dr. Sam thinks it could be scar tissue from my first tumor surgery years ago. Everything else was fine. Dr. Sam asked Bruce how he was and what protocol he was on. He said that Bruce looked "really good." So Bruce and I both had a good appointment with my oncologist!

Friday, 6/17:

Bruce and I walked at Horseshoe Lake today. I so admire his stamina! I just wish I could keep up with him!

Saturday, 6/18:

Bruce went back on his chemo pills this morning. Here we go again!

Despite being on chemo pills, Bruce and I went to Sean's and Colin's soccer games this morning and to a high school graduation party for a former student of mine this afternoon. Today was a full and happy day for both of us!

Monday, 6/20:

Bruce and Doug went to a baseball game in Philadelphia today—Doug's Christmas gift to Bruce. They left early and didn't get home til 8:30 p.m. Thankfully Bruce had a great day and felt fine after they got home! Baseball always makes Bruce happy!

Tuesday, 6/21:

Bruce started chemo again this morning. He's back on the strong stuff so we were there about four hours. His cancer markers and blood work continue to be fine and his weight is stable.

Thursday, 6/23:

Bruce, Doug, Gianna, and I went over to Chris and Jen's early this morning. Then we all left for Dutch Wonderland. We had a good trip and nice weather. We were there all day. The boys had a ball and Bruce did fine! From the Park we went out to dinner and then to our hotel. The end of a long but great day!

Friday, 6/24:

After breakfast, we all went to Hershey Park. We were there all day and everyone had a good time, especially the boys!

Saturday, 6/25:

Today we went to the Chocolate Factory. From there we went to lunch and to the outlets. After we got back to the hotel, Bruce, Doug, and I went for a long walk. We're doing a lot of walking and Bruce has been feeling fine throughout all of it!

Sunday, 6/26:

We left for home this morning after a very nice trip! Bruce actually enjoyed this one (As opposed to Disney when he couldn't do anything.)!

Tuesday, 6/28:

Bruce had an appointment with Dr. Carl's partner this morning. She said everything's fine but told Bruce not to "overdo it" when he told her about all the walking he does. Bruce has reached the limit for radiation so he won't have any more even if (God forbid.) something turns up down the line. It'll be back to chemo in that case. From that appointment we went to chemo. Bruce's cancer markers and blood work continue to be fine. He has to have an injection tomorrow to boost his white blood cell count as this heavy chemo does a number on white blood cells. The injection is supposed to make you feel like you have the flu for a couple of days. I hope Bruce will be okay with this, as he has been with everything else.

Wednesday, 6/29:

After my long dentist appointment, Bruce and I went to the Cancer Center for Bruce's injection. After we got home, Bruce went to the movies. Looks like the "flu like symptoms" haven't hit him yet!

Tuesday, 7/5:

Bruce and I went to the Cancer Center for his blood work—everything's fine. Of course, Bruce predicted it would be fine!

Wednesday, 7/6:

Bruce and I met Doug in Morristown this evening. We went out to dinner and then went to the library for Doug's book club, which he'd invited us to. Bruce and I enjoyed it and met a lot of nice people. One young woman had a purple pancreatic cancer shirt on. Her boss' father died from pancreatic cancer and she's very involved with PanCan. After the meeting, Bruce, Doug, and I talked with her for a little while. What are the odds we'd meet someone at the meeting with a connection to pancreatic cancer? The Universe does work in mysterious ways!

Sunday, 7/10:

Today was a full day for us! First we met Doug for breakfast. After we got home, we went to the high school track to walk. Then we went to see Chris as he leaves on a business trip today. Later, we went to the hospital to visit Bruce's brother, Wayne. From the hospital we went out to dinner. These are the days with Bruce that I value most—both of us feeling well and doing "normal" things. So I'm especially grateful for today.

Monday, 7/11:

Bruce and I picked Jake up this morning and took him to soccer camp in Newton. After it was over, we took him to a diner for lunch. Bruce has always gone to most of the boys games and always enjoyed watching them play. As soon as he was strong enough after his surgery, he was back on the sidelines for almost every one of the boys' games!

Tuesday, 7/12:

Bruce and I went to chemo this morning. All of his markers are good!

Wednesday, 7/13:

A day after chemo and Bruce was feeling great! So we took Jake to soccer camp and out to lunch again. We both enjoyed this special time with Jake!

Thursday, 7/14:

Bruce and I took a train from Iselin to D.C. today. Michael picked us up and drove us to our hotel. After we got settled, we went to Michael and Laura's for dinner. It was so nice to spend time with both of them and the boys. Judson and Dominic had fun climbing all over their Papa Bruce!

Friday, 7/15:

Bruce and I went with Michael and the boys to the Air and Space Museum. We all enjoyed it!

Saturday, 7/16:

Today was Judson's fourth birthday so Bruce and I helped with all the festivities. The party was outside and Bruce spent a little time playing baseball with Judson and his friends. It was a nice day—our last in Virginia before heading home tomorrow.

Tuesday, 7/19:

Bruce and I went to the Cancer Center for an appointment with Dr. Al plus chemo. Dr. Al's very pleased with Bruce's progress and said there is reason to be "encouraged." I was so happy and relieved to hear that! Bruce's white blood cell count was low due to the chemo so Dr. Al said to stop the chemo pills for now. Tomorrow, Bruce has to go back down for the shot that boosts white blood cells. Next week, he'll just go down for blood work. Two weeks after that, he'll have chemo and THAT'S IT! A month after Bruce's last chemo, he'll have a Cat scan. Then he'll be like me—Cat scans on a regular basis. Thank God Bruce has done so well and come so far!

Wednesday, 7/20:

Bruce and I attended our first Wage Hope meeting for pancreatic cancer. The people there were lovely and Bruce and I felt very comfortable being with them. We heard very sad stories of loved ones who'd passed from pancreatic cancer. But there were also a few long-term survivors (7, 10, and 11 years) and their stories were very uplifting (Especially since only 8% of pancreatic cancer patients survive five years after diagnosis.). Bruce offered to have his story put on their Face Book page so they took our picture after the meeting. I can't explain this meeting and these people adequately. It's something you'd have to experience.

Last week, Bruce went to May and Wayne's for dinner. I called May today and she told me how much they enjoyed Bruce's visit. May said that Bruce has so much energy he's like the "energizer bunny" (True!).

Sunday, 7/24:

Bruce and I went to a luncheon at St. Jude's. Several people came up to us to ask Bruce how he was doing. They all said how good he looks!

Monday, 7/25:

Todd, from Wage Hope, posted an article about Bruce and me, as well as a picture. Bruce and I really appreciated it. What's more, we got a lot of beautiful comments back—many calling us "inspiring." It was all very touching. All we want to do is to beat pancreatic cancer and to call attention to its cause along the way. By going to the Wage Hope meeting last week, we are on our way! WAGE HOPE!

Tuesday, 7/26:

Bruce and I went to the Cancer Center for his blood work. Everything continues to be fine! Dr. Al told Bruce he looks "great."

Wednesday, 7/27:

While Chris and Jen are away, Bruce is taking care of their cats, bringing in their mail, taking care of their garbage, and watering their plants. Chris said to me: "What would we do without Bruce?" Indeed! I hope we never have to find out!

Thursday, 7/28:

Bruce spent a long time at Chris and Jen's working on their lawn this morning—he mowed, weeded, trimmed, and watered. He also took care of their cats. After all of this, he went to the high school and walked four miles. He was gone from 6:30 a.m. to 1:30 p.m. Bruce is definitely back to normal!

Tuesday, 8/2:

Bruce and I went to chemo. His blood work and tumor markers were fine again. Next week is his last chemo (Hopefully for good!) and we're both very excited! After we got home, I emailed the family about next Tuesday. After Bruce's last chemo, he gets to ring the bell outside. Afterwards, we'll go out to dinner to celebrate.

Tuesday, 8/9:

A spectacular day!!!

Chris and Carol both texted this morning to wish Bruce good luck in the afternoon. Michael called to do Face Time to let Bruce know they were thinking of him.

Bruce and I went to his chemo treatment today—God willing, his last one ever! We brought a big tray of pastries for the staff. I wrote a note to Dr. Al and the staff thanking them for everything. Everyone was so happy for Bruce! When it was time for the bell ringing, May arrived first with balloons. Debbie, Michael, and Gianna came—also with balloons! Doug and Maureen and Henry came. Then Bruce rang the huge bell outside the Cancer Center. It was so loud I'm sure everyone inside heard it! We took pictures afterwards and then Bruce gave a little talk about his ordeal. He did a very good job and I was so proud of him! After that, we all went for an early dinner. It was a terrific celebration—everyone was beyond happy for Bruce (especially me)! I can't even put into words how grateful I am for how well Bruce and I are doing. May we both continue to do well going forward. Thank you, God!

Wednesday, 8/10:

Jen and I both posted pictures on Face Book from yesterday. I sent Melissa a message telling her how Bruce referenced Dylan in his speech yesterday. Bruce said how Dylan gave him the will to live because he wanted to do the 5K at the Dinosaur Stomp for Dylan. Melissa said it made her cry.

Bruce went to the Cancer Center for the shot to boost his white blood cells. He'll still be going down there on a somewhat regular basis: still better than going down for chemo!

Bruce and I went to the monthly Wage Hope meeting this evening. The people there are so inspiring—what they're doing for the cause of pancreatic cancer is so selfless.

Thursday, 8/11:

What a great day this was! Bruce, Chris, Michael C., and I went to the Barclay Center in Brooklyn to see Barbra Streisand in concert! The concert was wonderful! It gave me chills! I've always hoped to see Barbra Streisand in concert but never dreamed I actually would one day! (We saw a beautiful rainbow on our way to the concert—surely a sign of sunny days ahead!)

Sunday, 8/14:

Bruce, Carol, and I went down the Shore for a wedding and stayed overnight. It was a beautiful wedding but a very long day. God bless Bruce for doing all the driving and for staying out late at the wedding reception!

Tuesday, 8/16:

Bruce went for blood work this morning. Dr. Al said everything's good and that he'll see Bruce the end of September.

Wednesday, 8/17:

Bruce, Carol, Douglas, Michael and Laura and the kids, and I went to a Yankee game today. The Yankees lost (And Bruce is a Yankee fan.). By the time we got home around 6:00 p.m., Bruce felt light headed and had to lie down for a while. Thankfully, he was alright later on. Every time something like this happens, I can't help but think the worst.

Friday, 8/19:

This evening was my family birthday dinner at a restaurant in Denville. Bruce, Carol, all three boys, both daughters-in-law, and all five grandsons were there. It was a lovely evening and it was nice to be celebrated. The best gift I received this year will always be the best gift ever—Bruce's good health!

Monday, 8/29:

A friend of mine from high school sent me a private Face Book message today. He referred to Bruce and me as "real life heroes." I wrote back saying we're not heroes; we're just making the most of a difficult situation. He wrote back that he "begs to differ" with me and that Bruce and I are "heroes." As much as we appreciate that, we also know it's not true. The real heroes in this battle are the doctors, nurses, researchers, and all the children who have this dreaded disease. They're the heroes!

Saturday, 9/3:

Bruce and I drove forty minutes in order to be at Sean and Jake's soccer tournaments. Bruce really wanted to go. He loves supporting the boys at their games!

Sunday, 9/4:

Today was a beautiful day! Bruce and I had a baby shower at the house for Jen. Everything was perfect! But the best part came after almost everyone had left: Chris and Jen asked Bruce to be their baby's Godfather! I was stunned! Bruce was speechless and teary-eyed. What an honor! We're just thrilled. After everyone left, Bruce said he "survived everything for this moment—to be Godfather for my girl." He was so emotional and it was very sweet. Chris and Jen said that Bruce was their first and only choice for Godfather. What a perfect day this was!

Wednesday, 9/7:

Franco, from our Wage Hope group, emailed that he can't go to a health fair in Piscataway on Saturday and he asked if anyone could help out. Bruce and I finally have a free day so we volunteered to help. We've gotten involved in so many things since Bruce's diagnosis.

Thursday, 9/8:

Bruce went for his first haircut since last December! Since he lost most of his hair from chemo, this was an eventful day for us! Afterwards, we went to watch all three boys play tennis.

Friday, 9/9:

I went with Bruce to his three months' checkup with Dr. Steve. Dr. Steve was very pleased with Bruce's progress and how well he looks. He said Bruce's story is "truly inspiring." We've heard that a lot over the past several months but it meant even more to hear it from a doctor! Dr. Steve said you need "attitude and action" to get through something like this. He said he knew from his first time meeting Bruce that he had a wonderful attitude. He said he knew when he went to see him the day after surgery and Bruce was already out of bed and walking around the room that he had the right action to get through this. Going forward, Dr. Steve will monitor Bruce and make sure nothing is overlooked by the other doctors. We go back in January.

Saturday, 9/10:

Bruce and I volunteered at a health fair in Piscataway. Pietrina was in charge. Bruce was very good at talking about his surgery with a few people. He was able to encourage and give hope to them and their loved ones.

Sunday, 9/11:

Bruce and I went to May's surprise 70th birthday party this evening. It was a lovely evening! Bruce ate well and we even danced!

Tuesday, 9/13:

There was a birthday party for Bruce's Aunt Ann this afternoon. It was a barbecue at Bruce's cousin, Gary's, house. Aunt Ann turned 103 recently. God bless her!

Wednesday, 9/14:

Bruce went to the movies by himself. He loves his independence and not having to think about cancer. I'm just so happy for him!

Thursday, 9/15:

This evening, Bruce and I went to Morristown for dinner and then to the Community Theatre to see Regis Philbin and Don Rickles—a gift from Douglas. The show was very funny and we had such an enjoyable, relaxing evening.

Sunday, 9/18:

Bruce and I went to our second "Celebration of Life" for National Cancer Survivors' Day at Mayfair Farms. This is sponsored by St. Barnabas Medical Center. The dinner's always very good and the speeches are always very moving. This year, going meant even more to us since we are both cancer survivors!

Monday, 9/19:

I had my appointment with Dr. Sam today regarding my latest set of Cat scans. My scans haven't changed since three months ago. The nodule on my lung hasn't changed so that's good. My next scans are in December. Dr. Sam told Bruce he looked good and that he looked like he'd gained weight. I told Dr. Sam what a good job he did speaking at the Celebration of Life yesterday. He thanked me but seemed embarrassed. He and the other doctors we've gotten to know throughout our cancer journeys are all so humble.

Wednesday, 9/20:

A "random act of kindness" was bestowed on Bruce and me today. Michele's 90 year old mother crocheted purple hats for Bruce and me as her donation to Purple Stride. We'll wear them the day of our walk.

Bruce and I went to our Wage Hope meeting this evening. We were given two purple water bottles as we're presently the Purple Stride team with the most members (20)! Nice honor, especially since it's our first year. We heard of two more sad passings to this terrible disease this evening. But in general, the meeting was very uplifting and the people are friendly and supportive. I had no idea a year ago that we would be involved in anything like this.

Friday, 9/23:

Bruce and I went to Dr. Ken, Dr. Carl's replacement. Dr. Ken went over Bruce's records and examined him. He said Bruce is doing very well! He said with cancer, 90% of success is with the surgeon and 10% with the oncologists. I always believed the surgeons had the more difficult job.

After Dr. Ken, we went to our appointment with Dr. Al. We hadn't been at the Cancer Center since the beginning of August. It was as sad and as humbling as always. Dr. Al said that Bruce's blood work is "stellar"—no signs of cancer; white and red blood cells normal; no anemia; no diabetes. Everything is perfect! Dr. Al said that given how terrible pancreatic cancer is, Bruce is truly amazing! Our next appointment is the first week in December. Before we left, Dr. Al thanked Bruce for doing so well. He said that Bruce is his only patient with pancreatic cancer who's doing well and that Bruce gives him hope in treating patients going forward. What he said and how he expressed it was very moving.

After our appointment, we went to the treatment room (Ah, the stressful memories!) so Bruce's port could be flushed out. That only took a few minutes. Besides the wonderful news today, this also means that we can have our first Thanksgiving in three years without a shadow hanging over it. Last year it was Bruce's cancer and the year before it was mine. Plus, we have Baby Ella to look forward to around the same time. I feel like for the first time in a couple of years, I can breathe.

Thursday, 9/29:

Bruce and I went to watch all three boys play tennis today. They're all doing very well!

Friday, 9/30:

Bruce and I spent over four hours at one of our local Cancer Centers today. We volunteered with some of our Pancan friends to distribute information and to talk with anyone who stopped by.

Tuesday, 10/4:

Hopatcong's Mayor called this morning to talk to Bruce about designating 11/17 World Pancreatic Cancer Day in Hopatcong. Bruce had stopped in to talk to her about this one day but she was out.

Friday, 10/7:

Today we went to Sean's soccer game in Summit. Long drive but we always enjoy the boys' games!

Saturday, 10/8:

Bruce and I went to Colin's soccer game this morning. Afterwards, we went to Shop Rite and then to Planet Fitness so Bruce could rejoin the gym. This was huge for him! I'm so happy he's well enough to rejoin a gym—another sign of life returning to "normal."

Sunday, 10/9:

Bruce wasted no time getting back to the gym—he went today! It was his first time there since last December. He came home very satisfied with himself! I'm so happy for him. This was a huge achievement after what he's been through!

Wednesday, 10/12:

Bruce, Doug, and I went to Philadelphia today. We went to the Constitution Museum, had lunch, walked past Ben Franklin's grave, and toured Constitution Hall. After that, we drove to the Philadelphia Museum of Art where Bruce and Doug climbed the same steps Rocky climbed in his first movie. I thought it was a spectacular achievement for Bruce to be able to do this after what he's been through these past nine months. I got teary-eyed seeing Bruce make it to the top and walk down without any problems at all. He's simply amazing! I'm grateful Doug suggested this trip and that he did all those steps with Bruce! What a great day!

Thursday, 10/13:

Bruce went to the gym and came home with two dozen roses and a beautiful card for our anniversary, which is tomorrow. It'll be 27 years.

Wednesday, 10/19:

Bruce and I attended a workshop on communicating with your angels at Rosemary DeTroio's house. She runs a business in her home, "Hands of Light by Rosemary." Bruce and I have had other sessions with her but this was our first one on communicating with your angels. The other participants apparently received messages from their angels. Bruce and I didn't get anything. But here's the amazing part of this experience: After we left to go home, Bruce turned on the car radio. A beautiful song that neither of us had ever heard came on. It was called, "How to talk to the Angels." Talk about a sign and lots of goosebumps!

This evening, we went to our Wage Hope meeting. Despite the usual sad stories, the meeting was very uplifting.

Sunday, 10/23:

Bruce and I volunteered at Family Fun Day in Denville today. We worked with Pietrina, her husband, Anselmo, and Gordon. Pietrina's father died from pancreatic cancer. Gordon's father and college roommate both died from it. Today was another uplifting day of volunteering.

Thursday, 10/27:

Bruce and I went to Virginia this morning. When we got to Michael and Laura's, we got the happy news that Laura is pregnant! What a nice way to start our weekend with Michael, Laura, Judson, and Dominic!

Friday, 10/28:

This morning we met Laura at the house and followed her to the boys' school for their Halloween parade. I was so happy I got to see their parade for the first time. Afterwards, Laura went to work and Bruce and I went out to lunch and back to the hotel. Later, we went back to Michael and Laura's for dinner.

Saturday, 10/29:

After breakfast and using the hotel's gym, we went over to Michael and Laura's. We all went to Judson's soccer game. Later, Michael, Bruce, and I took the boys to Barnes and Noble. After we got home and had dinner, we took the boys to the playground. I took some cute pictures of Bruce playing with the boys on the equipment. Bruce is always such a good sport—nothing stops him from having fun!

Monday, 10/31:

This morning, Bruce and I went to Colin's Halloween parade. In the afternoon, we went back for Sean and Jake's parades. It's always fun seeing the boys in their costumes and in their parades!

Tuesday, 11/1:

Bruce's went to the Cancer Center to have his port flushed.

Wednesday, 11/2:

This evening, we went to a Town Hall meeting. Bruce received a Proclamation declaring 11/17 National Pancreatic Cancer Day in Hopatcong. They read the Proclamation and then called Bruce up to speak. He did a great job and I was very proud of him!

Friday, 11/4:

Bruce and I had another very good day volunteering at a cancer center. I loved talking with some of our Wage Hope friends there. I heard all about Michael's eleven year struggle with pancreatic cancer. It's unbelievable what he went through! You meet the most inspiring people at any cancer center.

Bruce's next Cat Scan is scheduled for 11/17, National Pancreatic Cancer Day! Bruce said that's a "good sign." I hope he's right!

Saturday, 11/5:

While Chris and family were at Sean's birthday party, Bruce spent three hours at their house blowing leaves in their backyard. God bless Bruce—his strength and stamina in light of all he's been through never ceases to amaze me!

Monday, 11/7:

Bruce and I met Doug at the Relay for Life in Parsippany. Bruce and I did the walk for survivors, which was very emotional for both of us. Then we did the walk for caregivers and even carried the banner! They had a special dinner for the survivors after the walks. Bruce had a rough time with the high temperatures and humidity. With the chemo he's on, extremes in temps really bother him. Aside from that, it was a long but worthwhile day!

Friday, 11/11:

Bruce spent a few hours at Chris and Jen's blowing their leaves again. He loves being able to help them when he can.

Saturday, 11/12:

Bruce spent most of today helping to set up for Purple Stride, which is tomorrow. He told me he did a lot of the "heavy work"—lifting and carrying boxes, setting up tables, etc. Bruce will do anything for this organization.

Sunday, 11/13:

This was an absolutely amazing day and one I'll never forget! Today was Purple Stride—the walk/run for Pancreatic Cancer. Ken Rosado from ABC News was the emcee. He asked Bruce how long he's been a survivor and wished him luck going forward. There were about 3,000 people there (Only 30 survivors, including Bruce.). The opening program was very moving. Lisa, from our Wage Hope group, and a two and a half year survivor, spoke and did an excellent job! After the program, it was time for our first 5K! Michael, Bruce, and I walked together. We all finished the Walk!

After we got home, it was time for our first "Purple Luncheon." Everyone from our team came, including Dylan! It was wonderful having Dylan here as he's been such an inspiration to Bruce. After lunch, Bruce gathered everyone in the living room and gave an impromptu speech about what he's been through, thanking everyone, and talking about how Dylan has helped him get through everything. What Bruce said was beautiful and heartfelt. Several people in the room got teary-eyed. I was really proud of Bruce and grateful for this perfect day!

Thursday, 11/17:

World Pancreatic Cancer Day.

Bruce had his first post-treatment Cat scan this morning. He wasn't nervous but I was! From the hospital we went to Urgent Care as I had a fever and sore throat. The doctor was new and when I told her about Bruce, her face dropped. She told me what I already know—that the statistics for survival are very bad. I told the doctor how well Bruce is doing and that he was sitting in the waiting room if she wanted to see for herself. I'm sure she was shocked to see how well Bruce looked (Most people usually are!).

Friday, 11/18:

Bruce went over to Chris and Jen's to blow their leaves again. If he's not working on our lawn, he's working on theirs!

Saturday, 11/19:

Disturbing early morning news: I got Bruce's Cat scan reports emailed to me. It appears that the stomach/pelvic one is okay but that something small showed up on the chest scan. They indicated it could be surgical or early stage metastatic disease. Back to worrying. We've been down this road before and it turned out to be surgical. Hopefully, that's all this is. This is not an easy journey we're on. And one never knows how it's going to end.

Monday, 11/21:

I left Dr. Al a message and he called back later on. He thinks Bruce's chest scan is just showing normal surgical swelling. He told me to contact Dr. Steve to get his opinion. If Dr. Steve thinks Bruce should go for a Pet scan, Dr. Al will order it. I immediately emailed Dr. Steve and he got right back to me. He was in Arizona and said he'll look at Bruce's scans on Monday, confer with Dr. Al, and then call me. I'll try not to worry about it until then.

Wednesday, 11/23:

While babysitting early this morning, I got an email from Dr. Steve. He'd already looked at Bruce's scans. He said that while he's "hopeful and optimistic," a Pet scan is warranted. Back to worrying.

Now the BIG NEWS: Baby Ella Mae, our first granddaughter, was born at 8:05 a.m. She's healthy and beautiful! Bruce, the boys, and I all got to meet Ella after we picked them up from school. She's so beautiful! Jen, despite having had a C section, is doing well and looks beautiful as always!

Thursday, 11/24:

Happy Thanksgiving! I have so much to be thankful for! We had a wonderful dinner with the family at the house!

Wednesday, 11/30:

Dr. Al's nurse called to tell us that my insurance company approved Bruce's Pet scan. Good news there! Later, the hospital called to schedule it for Friday morning. Here come the nerves again. Bruce finally admitted to being afraid of dying though he also said as soon as he gets those thoughts, he pushes them out of his mind. He told me that when I was first diagnosed, I said how I wouldn't be here to see our grandchildren grow up. I reminded Bruce that when he was in the hospital he said that he "wasn't ready" to leave me and the boys. We sure have been through a lot together! And the journey continues. . .

Friday, 12/2:

Bruce and I got to the hospital around 8:30 a.m. and didn't get out of there til around noon. Most of that time, I just sat and waited. I forgot how long a Pet scan takes (Even though I had one.). Now we await the results. I'm praying they'll be fine.

Saturday, 12/3:

Shortly after we got home from shopping, we got a call from the hospital. I got scared because I figured it must be Dr. Al calling with bad news since they usually don't call if it's good news. I was thankfully wrong!

Dr. Steve called asking if I'd gotten Bruce's Pet scan results. I told him we hadn't and asked if he had. He said yes and that the news was very good! Bruce's Pet scan is clear! Whatever appeared on the Cat scan has "resolved itself." Dr. Steve said Bruce is presently cancer free! Then he wished us a Merry Christmas. I thanked Dr. Steve and told him we would have a Merry Christmas now! Thank you, God!

Tuesday, 12/6:

Bruce and I went to his appointment with Dr. Al. Bruce's blood work and vitals were good. Dr. Al was very pleased to see Bruce looking and doing so well. He said when Bruce's Cat scan came back, he and Dr. Steve weren't sure if it was surgical or if "something" was going on. So Dr. Al shared the scans with his colleagues at the hospital and they all agreed that a Pet scan was warranted. Dr. Al said after the Pet scan came back and he discussed it with Dr. Steve, he asked Dr. Steve if he wanted to call us. Dr. Steve said that he would love to call us with the news. Dr. Al said he has a few other patients with pancreatic cancer and that Bruce is the only one doing well. He looked directly at Bruce and thanked him for giving him hope in treating such a terrible disease. He told us to celebrate every scan and every day. Bruce's next scan is in three months. After our appointment with Dr. Al, we went into the treatment room to have Bruce's port flushed. The nurses there were very happy to see Bruce. One of the nurses said they always looked forward to having Bruce there because he was always so positive and inspiring.

Monday, 12/19:

I got my first call since I applied to be a volunteer caregiver with Pancan. It was a woman from Pennsylvania whose sister has pancreatic cancer. We talked for a long time and she seemed relieved to have someone to talk to and to hear about Bruce's surgery and recuperation. She agreed to keep in touch. If I can do something good for someone in the same situation Bruce and I are in, then I will truly be blessed. As Robin Roberts says: "Make your mess your message."

Friday, 12/23:

Bruce took me to my appointment with Dr. Sam. Thankfully, my scans were fine. It'll be two years next month since my kidney surgery. Dr. Sam told Bruce he looked good. Bruce and I are blessed to have such caring oncologists!

Saturday, 12/24:

Bruce and I had a wonderful Christmas Eve dinner with Chris, Jen, the kids, Carol, and Douglas! Everything about the day was perfect! Of course, the kids' excitement was contagious and added to our glee. Best of all, our family had good news to celebrate—the gift of health!

Sunday, 12/25:

Merry Christmas! Bruce, Carol, and I visited the family at Gate of Heaven Cemetery and then we went over to Debbie and Michael's for dinner. It was another lovely day! Bruce and I are so blessed to have our health and our wonderful family. We are both very grateful!

PART THREE

2017: January through December

Friday, 1/06:

Bruce and I went for his check-up with Dr. Steve. The doctor said that since Bruce's biopsy was negative, his last Pet scan was fine and he works out and eats right, he has a good chance of beating this! Great news!!!

Wednesday, 1/11:

Bruce's surgery was one year ago today! Woo hoo!

Tuesday, 1/17:

Bruce went to the Cancer Center to have his port flushed. The nurses always look forward to seeing him!

Saturday, 2/25:

Ella's Christening! Bruce was so happy and so proud to be Ella's Godfather. They already have a special bond!

Monday, 2/27:

Bruce and I went to the Cancer Center for his blood work and to have his port flushed.

Saturday, 3/11:

Bruce and I marched in the St. Patrick's Day Parade in Morristown. Doug met us there and watched from the sidelines. This was Bruce's and Doug's second St. Patrick's Day Parade and my first. We marched with several of our Wage Hope friends for Pancan. After the parade, Bruce, Doug, and I went out for lunch. Happy St. Pat's Day!

Monday, 3/13:

This was not a good day at all. I accessed Bruce's scan results early this morning—they indicated a 1.2 cm mass near his stomach. They recommend a Pet scan. I put in a call to Dr. Al and emailed Dr. Steve. Dr. Al called later on in the day. He said that it's hard to tell what "this" is and that a Pet scan is warranted. In the evening, Dr. Steve emailed me to say that he spoke with Dr. Al and agrees that Bruce needs to have a Pet scan. He said there's definitely "something" there that wasn't on Bruce's Cat scan in December. He told me not to "jump to conclusions" and the fact that Bruce feels so well is a good sign. I hope so but I'm very nervous. I thought for sure this scan would be fine.

Thursday, 3/16:

I got very little sleep—too worried about Bruce. Jen sent me a picture of Ella "wearing purple for Papa Bruce." Later, I set up our Purple Stride team and used Ella's picture to announce it.

The hospital called about Bruce's Pet scan. Dr. Al ordered a scan from Bruce's skull to his thighs. He's covering everything this time. I'm trying to be calm.

Tuesday, 3/21:

Bruce and I got to the hospital by 7:30 a.m. We registered for his Pet scan and then spent the day and evening with Maureen and family (Maureen's in the same hospital.).

Wednesday, 3/22:

A devastating day. Maureen passed away this afternoon. And Bruce got very bad news this morning.

Bruce and I got to the hospital around 7:30 a.m. He went for his Pet scan while I stayed with Maureen. Dr. Al called while I was with Maureen, Henry, Kellie, and J.P. I took the call in the hall and got the terrible news that there is "cancer activity" that wasn't there in December. I'm devastated. I fell apart when I went back into Maureen's room. Bruce had gone to his car to get a drink. Thankfully, he wasn't there to witness my "meltdown." I was grateful to have Henry, Kellie, and JP there to hold me and talk to me. Then I went back into the hall and called Chris to tell him the news. I was still crying at that point. It's just terrible. When Bruce returned, I was calmer and able to tell him the news. As Henry had predicted, Bruce handled it better than I did. God only knows where we go from here.

Bruce and I left the hospital around 2:00 so we could bring Piper here and to give the family some "alone time" with Maureen. An hour later, JP called to tell me that she had passed. I lost my best friend of 40 years. I'm heartbroken. Rest In Peace, my dear friend. You were the BEST!

Thursday, 3/23:

Bruce took me to my appointment with Dr. Sam. Everything's fine. My next Cat scan is the end of June. I told Dr. Sam about Bruce. He was very sorry to hear it. He said that treatment depends on where the mass is and that they should do a biopsy. He said to let him know if there's anything he can do. I told him when I get the results of Bruce's Pet scan and we see the doctors, I'll make an appointment for a consultation with him. I really would like his opinion.

Friday, 3/24:

I got Bruce's Pet scan results emailed to me and it's not good. Bruce and I had his appointment with the new radiation oncologist, Dr. Ken. He didn't have access to the Pet scan disc, just the report. He said it "appears" to show a small, localized mass. He's certain Dr. Al will order a biopsy and chemo after that. I'm beyond scared but trying to be strong for Bruce. He continues to remain positive and optimistic but it's got to be bothering him deep down, especially after watching Bob die from colon cancer. I hate this disease so much! And I'm so scared.

Saturday, 3/25:

Bruce and I had a nice talk today about what may lie ahead. I'm a nervous wreck and very scared. He said he's not nervous or scared. He said he doesn't want to die but that he's not afraid of dying. He said he knows God and his angels will be with him and that when it does happen, he will see his family and mine in Heaven. I told Bruce he doesn't have to be strong or pretend to be strong for me. But I could tell from what he said and from his demeanor that he's not pretending about anything. As I told him, he truly is an amazing person. I'm not sure I totally appreciated that till all of this began.

Bruce and I went to St. Jude's for Mass this evening. When they prayed for the sick, they only prayed for Bruce. And when they prayed for the deceased, they only prayed for Maureen. I whispered to Bruce that even now he and Maureen are connected.

Tuesday, 3/28:

Dr. Steve talked with me and then with Bruce. He was in on a video conference this morning about Bruce. He said they're not sure what this nodule in Bruce's stomach is so he'll have to have a biopsy. If it's cancer, Bruce will be back on chemo.

Bruce and I had his appointment with Dr. Al today. He said twenty doctors were in on that video conference. The confusing part is that Bruce looks and feels good and isn't having any symptoms. Dr. Al scheduled the biopsy for Thursday.

Family and friends are calling, texting, or messaging to ask about Bruce.

Thursday, 3/30:

Henry and JP picked us up at 8:30 and took us to the hospital. They took Bruce in for his biopsy around 10:15. He was done around 11:15, at which time, Henry, JP, and I went into the recovery room. Bruce did well and looked good. The results should be in on Monday. We were in recovery for about an hour. Then JP went for the car and Henry and I followed Bruce, who was wheeled out of the hospital. Bruce was tired once we got home and ended up taking a two hour nap.

Monday, 4/3:

I walked around with both phones all day but no news. Bruce is very optimistic. I know that worrying isn't going to change the outcome or help in any way. But of course, I'll be nervous when I get that phone call. Bruce keeps asking if I'd heard anything so I know he's worried too. However, he did tell me (With a smile.) that no matter what happens, he'll help me through it!

Tuesday, 4/4:

I've used this word before and I sadly must use it again: this was a devastating day. Dr. Al finally called around 7:00 p.m. Bruce has stage four pancreatic cancer as it has metastasized into his stomach. I had the phone on speaker so Bruce could hear everything. Dr. Al wants Bruce to start chemo next week. Dr. Al gave me the name of a specialist at Weil Cornell in the City whom he wants me to call. I'm beyond devastated and so scared. Bruce is sad but is convinced he can beat this. I think he's more worried about me than himself. I didn't handle the news very well. The family has assured me that I won't be going through this alone. God bless all of them!

Wednesday, 4/05:

I was up all night—worrying and thinking. I'm so scared and so worried about Bruce. I reached Dr. Marie at Weil Cornell and we have an appointment on Tuesday.

Thursday, 4/6:

Jen wrote something beautiful about Bruce on Face Book. She said she "meant every word." Bruce is so loved.

I reposted the picture of our Purple Stride team on Face Book and wrote something about it. I mentioned that it has more meaning to me now than it did in November as Bruce has had a "setback." Several people commented. Bruce and I have a lot of prayers and support.

Friday, 4/7:

I got Bruce's schedule at the Cancer Center. We go there Wednesday for chemo counseling and then for chemo. The last time chemo was around three hours. This time it'll be four hours. Plus, Bruce will come home with a chemo pump for 48 hours. We'll go back down there on Fridays to have it removed. This is going to be a very difficult journey. Bruce continues to be positive and to look at this as another "challenge" to overcome. I wish I could be that strong.

Bruce took his car for service today. He told the men there about his illness. He told me that one of the guys hugged him. They all wished him well.

Saturday, 4/8:

At 3:00 a.m., Bruce woke up and wanted to talk. He said he didn't want "to scare" me but that he wants to ask the New York doctor what his prognosis is. He said he doesn't want to die but he's also not afraid to die. He said if he knows how much time he has it'll only make him fight harder (Amazing, right?!). I told him I think asking that can be a self-fulfilling prophesy. I suggested he ask the success rate of the new chemo and he agreed to that.

Sunday, 4/9:

Bruce and I went to Jake's soccer game this afternoon. On our way home, Bruce told me that when he was holding Ella (At Chris and Jen's, prior to the game.), she had her head on his shoulder and that three times she looked up into his eyes. He said he had a feeling that she was trying to tell him everything would be alright and that she needs him. It seemed to give him a great deal of peace. He said that while Ella was looking at him, he got chills throughout his entire body. Usually that's a sign that someone's soul is with you. I wish I knew if that's what it meant and whose soul it was. God bless Ella! As I told Chris and Jen, if Bruce makes it through this, it will partly be due to Ella!

Tuesday, 4/11:

Bruce and I met Doug in Denville and we took the train into the City. After sitting in Central Park for a while, we walked to Weil Cornell for our appointment. Bruce and I really liked Dr. Marie. She was very encouraging. The bottom line is that the mass is extremely small and Dr. Marie said with chemo for three months, Bruce should be able to beat this! It was the first time I felt hopeful. Bruce always had hope! Dr. Marie recommended the same type of chemo Dr. Al did, just not as strong. She recommended other things that she'll discuss with Dr. Al. Doug came in with us and took notes, which helped a lot. Only God knows what's going to happen down the line, but God answered my prayers today—Bruce isn't going anywhere anytime soon! Now I can breathe!

Wednesday, 4/12:

Bruce and I went to the Cancer Center today. We had counseling to explain the chemo regimen, side effects, and medicine and vitamins Bruce has to take. Dr. Al stopped in and said how sorry he is that Bruce is going through this. He said Dr. Steve also feels terrible for Bruce. We filled Dr. Al in on Dr. Marie and he's doing everything she's requested. A piece of Bruce's pancreas was sent out for genetic testing. Bruce will have chemo for four hours every other week. On the off week, he'll go down for blood work. He'll wear a chemo pump for 48 hours every time he has chemo. That goes on once chemo is completed.

Sunday, 4/16:

Today is Easter Sunday. The chaplain from St. Clare's said Mass at St. Jude's. Afterwards, Bruce told him the latest with his health issues. Father Paul said he'll pray for Bruce. Despite the distressing turn of events, Bruce still enjoyed our Easter dinner with the family!

Wednesday, 4/19:

Bruce went to the Cancer Center by himself for his blood work. He said everything's fine! He also went to our Wage Hope meeting by himself.

Thursday, 4/20:

I missed a special Wage Hope meeting last night. Since April is volunteer month, they honored a few people with awards. One was for Bruce and me for being the "volunteer purple passion duo." We got a framed certificate and a few little gifts. Bruce said he gave an impromptu speech, which I'm sorry I missed. He said he teared up while he was speaking. I'm so glad Bruce had the opportunity to do this!

Monday, 4/24:

Bruce and I walked two miles at Horseshoe Lake. He could've gone longer but I had had enough!

Wednesday, 4/26:

Bruce had chemo today. Dr. Al said since Bruce left the hospital cancer free and was cancer free for a year he really thought Bruce was going to beat this. I asked what he meant when he said this was "incurable, just treatable." He said that since they can't operate on this mass, they can only treat it. Dr. Al said that vitamin D infusions done three times a week are helpful with pancreatic cancer. So we agreed to do it. From here on in, Bruce will have scans every three months. Any new masses will be dealt with on an on-going basis. I don't like the sounds of this at all. I'm afraid this is not going to have a happy ending. I just hope Bruce will be here as long as possible. I also hope I'm strong enough to face whatever lies ahead.

Thursday, 4/27:

Bruce was a little nauseous and light-headed all day. He mostly rested.

Friday, 4/28:

Bruce went to the Cancer Center to have his pump removed and to get his first infusion of Vitamin D. He felt fine today and said everything went well. Bruce told me he thinks he's "going through this" in order to help other people through it. Then he asked if there were classes he could take to learn to speak better in front of people. He's dealing with one of the worst cancers there is and he's thinking about helping others! That's Bruce.

Saturday, 4/29:

Bruce felt light-headed today. He mowed the lawn but then rested. It was sad and scary to see him just lying there not even able to watch t.v. He felt better later on so we went out to dinner with J.P. (J drove.). Bruce was okay but didn't eat much.

Sunday, 4/30:

Bruce and I attended our first Purple Light at a camp in Warren. They had a big screen set up with photos of those who've passed and also, of the survivors from our Wage Hope group, including a picture of Bruce and me from Purple Stride. Todd did a beautiful job organizing this very special though emotional evening.

Monday, 5/1:

Bruce went to the Cancer Center for his Vitamin D infusion. He does this three times a week.

Tuesday, 5/2:

This evening, Bruce went to a cancer support group in Morristown. He came home with a lot of information. While he was there, Lisa, from our Wage Hope group, called. She's a three year pancreatic cancer survivor. She wanted to know the latest with Bruce. It was so good for me to talk about everything with Lisa. I'm blessed to have such support.

Wednesday, 5/3:

This morning, Bruce bought several purple plants and planted them out front. He also bought purple chimes, which he hung out on the deck. Purple is the color for pancreatic cancer.

Bruce had an appointment with Dr. Al this afternoon and then he had his Vitamin D infusion. Dr. Al gave us very distressing news. Bruce will be on some form of chemo for the rest of his life. Since his cancer is malignant, stage four, and inoperable, he will need chemo to keep him alive. Bruce was very upset at first. He'd already been planning another bell ringing and celebration. There will be none of that now. The more we discussed it the better Bruce felt. He's hopeful he'll be alright and that the chemo won't be as strong down the line. I'm just heartbroken. Dr. Al got the results of Bruce's pancreas back and it didn't show any abnormalities or genetic markers.

Sunday, 5/7:

Bruce went to the health and wellness fair at Met Life Stadium to volunteer with our Wage Hope group. He was there all day. Despite what's going on, Bruce is still volunteering and helping others!

Tuesday, 5/9:

Bruce wanted to go to a Toastmasters' meeting this evening. He was hoping he could join and learn to be a better speaker. I went along to keep him company. It was interesting and everyone was very nice but Bruce thinks it's a little too advanced for him. I'd have to agree. They do debates and contests. Bruce just wants to learn how to give a decent speech.

Wednesday, 5/10:

Bruce's chemo lasted almost six hours today. His blood work was fine. He got a healing massage while he was getting chemo. The masseuse remembered Bruce and said she was sorry he was back but that she was very happy to see him again. Everyone loves Bruce!

Friday, 5/12:

When I left for Colin's Mother's Day Tea at his school, Bruce left for an appointment with Dr. Steve and then to the Cancer Center for his Vitamin D and to have his chemo pump removed. I felt terrible (and a little guilty) about missing Dr. Steve's appointment. Bruce said that Dr. Steve said he looks good. Bruce is now finished with Dr. Steve. We'll both miss seeing him. He's such a kind, caring doctor. Bruce brought home his blood work from the Cancer Center. His tumor markers are high but I'm not sure how bad it is. We'll find out on Wednesday. There's always something to worry about.

Saturday, 5/13:

Bruce was sick all day today. He couldn't go to Dylan's Dinosaur Stomp but he kindly drove me to the firehouse, where it was being held, since it poured all day. A lot of people at the firehouse asked me where Bruce was and how he was doing.

Monday, 5/15:

Happy Birthday, Bruce!!! He spent the day at the Sands in Pennsylvania with the Seniors. He was gone all day, he enjoyed himself, and he even won $117! I was so happy he had such a great day! He deserved it!

Wednesday, 5/17:

Bruce and I went for his vitamin D infusion and to meet with one of the physician assistants. We got very disturbing news—Bruce's cancer markers are triple what they should be! I was beyond upset! I asked if this means the chemo isn't working. The physician assistant just said we'd have to talk to Dr. Al about it next Wednesday. Bruce also lost weight, which I could see. He's not eating much at all. Despite all of this, we still went to our monthly Wage Hope meeting.

Thursday, 5/18:

This evening was Sean's spring concert. The gym was very hot and Bruce had to go outside to feel better. Extremes in temperature affect him.

Sunday, 5/21:

This morning Bruce and I went to a beautiful Mass for our former pastor's fiftieth anniversary as a priest. Afterwards, there was a reception for him in the church hall. Several people came over to us to ask how Bruce was feeling.

Wednesday, 5/24:

Bruce and I met with Dr. Al prior to chemo. Dr. Al said that Bruce's tumor markers are very high. He said they usually plateau mid-treatment and then drop by the end of treatment. Today was Bruce's fourth chemo treatment of this cycle. The real test will be Bruce's first post-treatment Cat scan. His sixth and last treatment of this cycle was scheduled for the week we're away so he'll have it the following week. Dr. Al informed us that insurance companies will no longer pay for vitamin D infusions because they're considered experimental and not FDA approved. They would cost us $300 per week. I told Bruce he had to make the decision and he said absolutely no to paying for this out of pocket. So we're reluctantly stopping the vitamin D infusions. Bruce got a much needed massage during chemo. We were gone a little over six hours; it was a long, distressing day.

Saturday, 5/27:

Bruce was fine today! It was the first time in four chemos (this round) that he wasn't fatigued, light-headed, and nauseous. I was so happy he felt well enough to go to Bianca and Gianna's graduation/birthday party.

Wednesday, 5/31:

Bruce and I went to the Cancer Center for his blood work. It's fine but that doesn't indicate the tumor markers.

Sunday, 6/4:

Today, Bruce and I worked at the Denville Street Fair. Our New Jersey Pancan Affiliate had a table there and Bruce and I helped out with a few of our Wage Hope friends. Bruce had an opportunity to talk to a few people with pancreatic cancer connections. He's so good at talking to people and sharing all that he's been through. He always says he "Just wants to be able to help one person." I always tell him he's helping a lot more than just one person!

Wednesday, 6/7:

Today was chemo #5 for Bruce. His blood work and weight were good. He was so cold during chemo that I had to put two heated blankets on him. He also always has a runny nose during chemo. Five hours later, after we'd gotten home, Bruce only ate peaches and applesauce. He took the anti-nausea pills but still threw up a couple of times. It was so sad listening to him vomiting as it's another sign of this terrible disease.

Thursday, 6/8:

Bruce threw up several times last night and this morning. Throughout the day, he gradually got better.

Saturday, 6/10:

Bruce, Doug, and I did the American Cancer Association's Relay for Life in Parsippany today. Another 5K for the three of us!

Sunday, 6/11:

Best news ever: Laura had a baby girl around 8:00 p.m.—Anna Katharine Filomena! She was 8 lbs., 7 oz. and is absolutely beautiful!

Tuesday, 6/13:

Bruce and I attended our first PanCan Leadership breakfast at a hotel in Summit. The speakers were wonderful! Bruce and I were honored to have been invited to this event!

Wednesday, 6/14:

Bruce had blood work today and an appointment with Dr. Al. Dr. Al said again how terrible he felt when Bruce's last Pet scan indicated a new cancer. He said that he thought Bruce would be the one person to beat this devastating cancer. I told him he still might! After Bruce's next chemo treatment (#6 of this cycle), he'll have a Cat scan and then another cycle of chemo. The tumor markers were tested today but the results won't be in until tomorrow afternoon. Dr. Al said again that there's no cure for Bruce. The goal is to treat him and keep him alive as long as possible. He said we also need to hope that a new discovery opens up along the way.

Thursday, 6/15:

I texted Dr. Al about Bruce's tumor markers and he got right back to me. Thankfully, Bruce's markers have gone down from 2,859 the beginning of May to 884 yesterday! Still high but much better—a sign that the chemo is working. Thank you, God!

Sunday, 6/18:

Bruce and I drove to Washington, D.C. for Pancreatic Cancer Advocacy Days. We met lots of people in purple shirts in the lobby. Every

State was represented! It was so good for Bruce to talk to survivors and family members.

Later, we took a taxi to Michael and Laura's and stayed for dinner. Then we took a taxi back to the hotel. After we got settled in our room, Bruce went to the lobby for a PanCan "greet and meet."

Monday, 6/19:

Today was day one of Advocacy Days—truly an amazing experience! While I had breakfast in a huge room with over 600 people, Bruce had breakfast in another room with 99 other survivors. He truly benefited from all of the people he met there! After breakfast, we heard several speeches and then sat in on work sessions that we had signed up for. One of those sessions was "How to Tell Your Story." It was a small group but we heard the saddest stories. Bruce got up to tell his story and they asked me to join him. I hadn't expected to talk but I did. Later, PanCan posted it on their Face Book page. This was quite a memorable day!

Tuesday, 6/20:

Day #2 of Advocacy Days—Capitol Hill! After breakfast and a couple of speeches, we headed over to Congress. Once there, our day was full and exhausting! First we met with Senator Menendez' aides. Senator Menendez showed up briefly. In his office, Bruce sat around the conference table and I sat behind him. Bruce and others got to tell their stories. Bruce did a very good job. From there, we walked over to Senator Booker's office and spoke with his aide. It was pretty much a repeat of what went on in Menendez' office. Last, we headed over to Congressman Frelinghuysen's office and met with his aide.

After Bruce and I got back to the hotel, we headed over to Michael and Laura's. We stayed in Virginia for the next four days. What a great week we had—advocating for pancreatic cancer and visiting family!

Tuesday, 6/27:

Kristin, from PanCan in California, called us this evening for a story she's writing about survivors' experiences in D.C. When she heard I'm a cancer survivor and that I was also at Advocacy Days, she asked to interview me too. We talked for a half hour and it went very well. Bruce and I were honored that we'd been asked to be included in Kristin's blog.

Wednesday, 6/28:

Bruce and I went to the new Cancer Center in Mt. Lakes for chemo. The new facility is larger and much more spacious than the other one, which helps in the waiting room as well as in the chemo room. We told a couple of the nurses and Dr. Al about Advocacy Days. Dr. Al would like Bruce back on vitamin D if insurance will approve it. I'll look into it again. Bruce was very sick tonight. It's so sad to see him like this and not be able to do anything to help him.

Thursday, 6/29:

Bruce threw up again this morning. I felt so sorry for him. He stayed in bed most of the morning and then took me to my appointment with Dr. Sam. I felt awful that Bruce had to drive—he didn't look well and his face was red. He brought his bucket in case we had to pull over (We didn't.). In true Bruce fashion, he said it was "good to get out of the house." Usually Bruce comes in with me to see Dr. Sam but this time he stayed in the waiting room. Thankfully, I got very good news: my scans were clear! Dr. Sam asked how Bruce was doing. I filled him in and showed him a print-out of Bruce's chemo. Dr. Sam said it's exactly the regimen Bruce should be on. I asked him about vitamin D infusions. He said there's no evidence that they work and that Bruce is getting exactly what he needs with the chemo he's on.

Friday, 6/30:

Thank God, Bruce was fine today—back to "normal"—working outside, going to the Deli to meet his friends, and walking. Bruce also went to the Cancer Center to have his chemo pump removed. A good day for Bruce!

Wednesday, 7/5:

Bruce and I had eye doctor appointments this afternoon. When Bruce was in with our doctor, he told him about his cancer and all he's been through. When the doctor came in to me, he told me that "Bruce really has a story to tell." Perhaps one day Bruce and I will tell his story in some form so that others might benefit from his cancer journey.

Monday, 7/10:

Bruce and I went to the hospital this morning for his Cat scans. No word on how they went. I feel like I always live in a state of anxiety.

Wednesday, 7/12:

Today was a terrible, heartbreaking day. I woke up around 4:30 (My average these days.) and checked my phone. There was an email about Bruce's scans. I nervously read through both scans and was devastated by what I'd read. The mass in Bruce's abdomen has doubled from two to four centimeters—after three months of chemo. I couldn't believe it! On the positive side, there's no metastasis. I had no choice but to tell Bruce. He was, of course, disappointed. He was hoping the mass would have decreased by now and that chemo could be reduced. After I told him, Bruce went to recycling, walked two miles on the high school track, and then walked a friend's dog. If this doesn't show what an amazing, positive, inspiring, and strong person Bruce is I don't know what does!

Bruce and I went to the Cancer Center and met with Kay, one of the physician assistants. Dr. Al wants Bruce's treatment to remain the same for two months and then to have the scans repeated. Kay said the fact that the mass has grown is, of course, "unfortunate." But the good news is that there's no metastasis. Bruce's tumor markers have gone down a little, his blood work is fine, and he continues to look and feel good. After that we went into the treatment room for the next four hours.

All Bruce ate after we got home was applesauce. Then he began vomiting and that continued til about 1:00 a.m. It was heartbreaking. I couldn't sleep and I couldn't help him. All I could do was lie there, listening to him throwing up. This is so hard on both of us. I'm just numb.

Thursday, 7/13:

Bruce just rested today. My heart breaks for him.

Friday, 7/14:

Bruce felt much better today and was back to his normal self! He and I went to the Cancer Center so he could have his pump removed. He was wearing his "Whipple Survivor" sweatshirt and a woman who had the same surgery talked to us about her experience with the Whipple, having pancreatic cancer, and then being operated on for stomach cancer. It's always encouraging to talk with cancer survivors.

Monday, 7/17:

Bruce started talking about the growth in his tumor today. He doesn't understand why this thing has grown despite three months of chemo. He said he doesn't want chemo, especially the pump, if it's not helping him. He also said he'd like to go back to Dr. Maria and get her opinion. I could tell how hard this is on him, despite how positive he always is. After all, this is his life.

Tuesday, 7/18:

Bruce went to the movies by himself today. He's back to his usual positive self!

Wednesday, 7/19:

After Bruce's blood work, we talked with Dr. Al. He said that while the growth of Bruce's tumor is "worrisome," it's not necessarily the cancer spreading. He said since Bruce's cancer markers are down and he continues to look and feel good, this could just be an inflammation or swelling. That's why he wants to do two months of chemo and then new scans. After that, he'll consult with Dr. Maria. If, God forbid, this is the cancer spreading, then the chemo is no longer working. In that case, the next step is immunology and trials. I prayed for a little encouraging news and we got it!

Saturday, 7/22:

Today, Bruce talked about how he's hoping the next Cat scan will show that the mass has decreased but that he's not counting on it. I told him no matter what, we're not going to "roll over and play dead." We'll then look into immunology and trials. Of course, I'm praying it doesn't come to that.

Wednesday, 7/26:

Today Bruce had chemo #8. His blood work was fine. They tested for his tumor markers and those results should be in tomorrow. Thankfully, Bruce wasn't sick at all after we got home! Yay, Bruce!

Thursday, 7/27:

Dr. Al texted me with very good news: Bruce's markers are down from 884 in June to 447 yesterday! They started at 2,859! The CA19 markers for a person without cancer is around 35.

Friday, 7/28:

Bruce had his chemo pump removed today—that always makes him feel good!

Sunday, 7/30:

We hosted a birthday party for Judson today. The family came up for a barbecue and party. Bruce felt dizzy and light-headed and ended up going to bed at 7:00 p.m.

Tuesday, 8/1:

Bruce had blood work this afternoon. He lost five pounds—not good.

Wednesday, 8/2:

A long but wonderful day! Bruce, Carol, Doug, and I took the Path into the City. We went for lunch and then Bruce and I went to Schubert's Theatre while Carol and Doug went to another theatre. Bruce and I saw Bette Midler in "Hello Dolly." We both loved it! Afterwards we met up with Carol and Doug and took the subway to the Oculus. We did a lot of walking and a lot of stair climbing but it was worth it! It's beautiful there! We ate dinner at a place in the Oculus. Afterwards we took the Path back to Jersey City and then headed home. Bruce and I both enjoyed this break from medical "stuff"—a day to just be "normal" and to have fun!

Wednesday, 8/9:

Bruce had an appointment with Dr. Al and chemo #9. Dr. Al said again how upset he was when he realized Bruce's cancer had spread. He said everything went so perfectly with Bruce for over a year and that he thought Bruce would be the "poster boy" for beating pancreatic cancer. Dr. Al said there's still a lot to learn about pancreatic cancer. He said if Bruce's tumor markers continue to go down then he'll wait til after chemo #12 to do scans. If not, he'll do them after chemo #10, which is in two weeks. We were at the Cancer Center for around five hours. Bruce was nauseous after we got home and threw up on and off till around 3:00 a.m. It's so sad to see him going through this. He's such a kind, caring person and deserves a life as good as he is.

Friday, 8/11:

Bruce had his chemo pump removed today. Afterwards he walked two miles on the high school track. By the time he got home, he was very tired and lay down for a while. I started worrying that something was wrong. Even after he got up, I asked him several times if he was okay. That's what's so difficult about this journey of ours—I never know what's "normal" and what's cancer related.

Monday, 8/14:

Chris posted an update on Face Book about Bruce. He's gotten over 100 responses, including several beautiful comments. Bruce continues to inspire a lot of people and it's heartwarming to read their comments.

Wednesday, 8/16:

Bruce and I went for his blood work today. It was perfect!

Sunday, 8/20:

Early this morning, Bruce, Doug, and I took the train to Port Authority. First we had breakfast in the City. Then Doug and I went to Madison Square Garden for a mass meditation. Bruce walked around the City for an hour and a half and said he enjoyed spending time by himself. After lunch, we walked to the High Line and did the long walk there in the summer heat. Bruce really enjoyed it! I'm always grateful when Bruce gets to have a day like today! And God bless him for doing so much walking!

Monday, 8/21:

Today's my birthday and Bruce got me a beautiful card and a dozen red roses. The best gift he gave me, however, was to be here to spend this birthday with me!

Wednesday, 8/23:

Bruce had chemo #10 this morning. Dr. Al said he'll let us know tomorrow about Bruce's cancer markers. He'd like to wait till after chemo #12 to do the next set of scans. Bruce's blood work was fine again. They gave him a shot to prevent him from freezing and then sweating during chemo. Whatever this shot was it did the trick! He didn't need the blanket I'd brought with me or the ones they have there. Nor did he alternate between freezing and sweating. They're going to give Bruce this same shot every time he has chemo. Bruce even felt better once we got home— no lightheadedness this time. He did throw up twice but still felt good! Hopefully, we'll get good news tomorrow about his markers.

Thursday, 8/24:

I called the cancer Center about Bruce's markers. They've gone up from 447 to 494. Not much but still discouraging. Kay (P.A.) said that Dr. Al said this is "just a hiccup" and no reason to become discouraged. He still wants to wait til after chemo #12 to repeat the scans. Yesterday, Bruce told Kay he was hoping the numbers would go down to 100. She told me how positive Bruce always is. I told her he's the "eternal optimist." She said that's why they all love him down there. As for Bruce, he was disappointed but didn't let it get him down. And our fight continues!

Friday, 8/25:

Bruce and I went to the Cancer Center to have his pump removed. Then we went out to lunch. We try to squeeze in as much "normalcy" into our lives as we possibly can!

Saturday, 8/26:

After we got home from Jake's soccer game today, Bruce had a stomachache. One of the many problems with cancer is that when anything is bothering you, you can't help but think the worst. When Bruce said his stomach hurt, I went straight to the mass in his abdomen, though I didn't voice my concerns.

Monday, 8/28:

Bruce and I did a yoga meditation app I'd put on my phone. Bruce saw shades of white and orange going in and out.

Tuesday, 8/29:

Bruce and I volunteered at a Cancer Center with Lisa today. It's always good to give back to our Wage Hope group, which does so much for so many, including us.

Wednesday, 8/30:

Bruce and I went to the Cancer Center for his blood work and an appointment with one of the nurse practitioners. Bruce's blood work was fine and the NP didn't seem concerned about Bruce's tumor markers going up a little. She said a lot of things can affect them and that they do tend to fluctuate.

Thursday, 8/31:

Bruce and I did the yoga meditation app today. Once again, he saw colors. I think he's on a much higher spiritual plane than I am because I don't see anything!

Saturday, 9/1:

Bruce and I took Sean, Jake, and Colin out to lunch and then to Barnes and Noble's, where we bought books for them and Ella. After we got back to the house, we enjoyed playing with Ella—especially Bruce, whom Ella clearly adores!

Sunday, 9/2:

We held our last family barbecue of the season today. Bruce and I always enjoy having our family up here. I hope we will both be well enough next year to have a lot more get-togethers.

Wednesday, 9/6:

Today was chemo #11. We met with one of the Physician Assistants. She said Bruce's blood work was fine. I told her about having to push chemo #12 back a week due to the Christening. She said that's fine and that she'll take care of it.

Thursday, 9/7:

Bruce felt good all day—he wasn't nauseous at all!

Friday, 9/8:

Bruce had his chemo pump removed. This was only the second time that Bruce wasn't sick after chemo. That's the good news. The bad news is that he has a terrible cough, especially at night. I'm starting to really worry about it as a lot of cancers settle in the lungs.

Saturday, 9/9:

Bruce coughed most of the night so we went to Urgent Care this morning. Thankfully, the doctor said Bruce's chest is clear and that this is most likely viral. He put Bruce on cough medicine, a decongestant, and nasal spray for the daytime, and Robitussen with Codeine for at night. Bruce just rested once we got home.

Wednesday, 9/13:

Bruce and I went to our Wage Hope meeting this evening. We got a purple pumpkin for having the most Purple Stride team members so far. Purple Stride is in November.

Friday, 9/15:

Bruce had blood work and an appointment with Dr. Al this morning. His blood work was fine. Dr. Al will schedule the next set of scans for October ninth. He said if the scans show that Bruce is stable, he will continue with the same chemo transfusions and schedule. Bruce was hoping they'd be reduced. I never expected that. If, God forbid, the cancer has spread, then chemo will be stopped since that would mean it's no longer effective. In that case, Dr. Al would discuss immune therapy with

Dr. Maria. Dr. Al wants Bruce to go back on the vitamin D infusions so he gave us a script for it. When he got up to leave, Dr. Al said to Bruce: "I want so much to be able to help you. You're such a good guy and I want so badly to help you." In typical Bruce fashion, he said: "You ARE helping me—I'm going to beat this!" I just asked Dr. Al to never give up on Bruce and he said he never would.

After lunch, we went back to the Cancer Center for meditation. It was an hour and was very good—especially for Bruce as once again he saw different colors and images.

Sunday, 9/17:

While Bruce, Chris, and I were at a Paul McCartney concert at Madison Square Garden, I checked my phone and saw a text from Dr. Al. Bruce's tumor markers have gone down from 497 to 387! Dr. Al said this is "great news"! I was thrilled and quickly showed the text to Bruce and Chris. This was a spectacular evening on so many levels!

Friday, 9/22-Sunday, 9/24:

Bruce and I and the rest of our New Jersey family were in Virginia this weekend for Anna's Christening, which was on Sunday. I'm grateful Bruce was well enough to do all of the driving as well as visiting with Michael, Laura, Judson, Dominic, and Anna.

Wednesday, 9/27:

Bruce had an appointment with Kay this morning. His blood work was fine. After we saw Kay, Bruce had four hours of chemo. He felt good throughout it. After we got home, he wasn't weak, nauseous, or lightheaded. It was wonderful!

Wednesday, 10/4:

Bruce and I did yoga at the Cancer Center. After that, he had his blood work, which was fine.

Thursday, 10/5:

Bruce spoke about pancreatic cancer and Purple Stride at this morning's Seniors' meeting. Henry wanted me to stand with Bruce, which I did. But Bruce didn't need me as he did a great job on his own! I was very proud of him! Two people came up to me afterwards to tell me that family members were recently diagnosed with pancreatic cancer. If the info and support I could offer these individuals is the only thing that comes of Bruce's talk, then it was indeed a success!

As if this wasn't enough excitement for one day, Bruce and I went to see Barry Manilow in concert at Prudential, in Newark, this evening. Bruce and I have been to several Manilow concerts and have always enjoyed them!

Sunday, 10/8:

Bruce had an amazing QHHT session with Nicky today. She put him into a semi-hypnotic state. His journey took him to a place Bruce called Heaven. He said it was "big, beautiful, and very quiet." He said the people there were always smiling. Bruce said he saw dogs there—ours and some he watched while pet-sitting. He also said he saw his brother, Bob, and best friend, Roger, both of whom had passed. They told Bruce they missed him but that they'll see him again one day. Bruce said that my parents and some of my aunts and uncles were together in another room. Bruce said he felt like he "was back home." Our family members knew about Bruce's illness and said that they are always praying for him. They told Bruce that they will see him again one day and that when they do, they will be there to greet him. Bruce said there were a lot of angels around him while he was in "Heaven." He said we have angels in Heaven and on Earth. He said that Ella was one of his angels in Heaven who came to Earth through Jen and is now one of Bruce's angels on Earth. God said Bruce will know in time why she was sent to him. Bruce felt his body begin to leave Heaven and float downwards. He felt that he was floating through the clouds and down into a beautiful forest that was very green and had lots of animals there. He said he held a rabbit, which was the softest thing he'd ever felt. Bruce felt his body come down to Earth. He said this session was "one of the best things" he's ever done. Nicky taped the session so I heard all of it. It was impossible not to believe. I'm so grateful to Nicky for doing this with Bruce. What a gift she gave him!

Monday, 10/9:

Bruce had his Pet scan this morning. For me, it's waiting for around two hours in the waiting room. And now the harder part begins—waiting for the results.

Wednesday, 10/11:

A very good day indeed! I got a copy of Bruce's Pet scan results this morning. I read that his abdominal mass had shrunk from 4 cm to 1.5 cm. I was thrilled! Later on in the afternoon, we had an appointment with Dr. Al and he confirmed what I'd read. He said it's "miraculous" for a malignant, stage 4 mass to decrease this much over a span of six months. He was almost as happy as we were! Besides all the prayers and Bruce's positive attitude, this means that the chemo is working. So he'll be on the same regimen for six more cycles and then have new scans. Thank you, God!

Bruce and I had a Wage Hope meeting this evening. Everyone was very happy to hear Bruce's news. So were all the family and friends I texted/ messaged/emailed/or called.

Friday, 10/13:

Bruce and I went to meditation at the Cancer Center. As always, he saw colors and objects while meditating. He gets a great deal of comfort out of meditation and yoga. I'm sure Bruce would've never considered either one if he hadn't gotten cancer.

Saturday,10/14:

Today was another day of "Waging Hope"! Bruce and I volunteered at Kinnelon Days. Pietrina, Anselmo, and Pat were also there. It was such a worthwhile day! Today was also wedding anniversary #28 for Bruce and me! He bought me a lovely necklace at one of the booths at the Fair. Pietrina couldn't believe we spent our anniversary volunteering (It was truly our pleasure.).

Wednesday, 10/18:

Bruce and I met with Dr. Al this morning. He said if the next set of scans shows no cancer, then he'll put Bruce on a maintenance program of chemo. That would be great! Bruce had chemo #1 (of six) for this new cycle. He did very well during and after treatment. As always, Bruce cheered up a couple of patients by talking to them and encouraging them (He literally walks around with his infusion pole so he can talk to different patients.). The head nurse said when she hears Bruce's voice she knows he's helping someone. All of the nurses have noticed what Bruce does and have commented on it. One of them said the whole "aura" of the Cancer Center shifts positively whenever Bruce walks in. How great is that?!

Thursday, 10/19:

Bruce was very tired all day today. We had registered to attend a three hour dinner/seminar on cancer but were unable to go to it.

Friday, 10/20:

Bruce had his pump removed and then went to meditation. He had another incredulous experience of "floating upwards towards the clouds."

Sunday, 10/22:

What a fun day today was! Bruce and I went to the Giants' game, compliments of Rush Limbaugh and his wife. We stayed in his VIP suite, along with others from our Wage Hope group and a few people from our NYC affiliate. Everything was free and the Box was beautiful! We were treated like celebrities! Bruce received three gifts from the Limbaughs and a lovely, personal note from them. Since Rush's father-in-law passed from pancreatic cancer, he and his wife want to raise awareness about it as well as bring joy to survivors. Speaking on behalf of Bruce, they sure brought joy to him today (Except that the Giants lost.)!

Tuesday, 10/24:

Bruce took me to my six month check-up with Dr. Lee today. Dr. Lee asked about Bruce so I filled him in on things. He said, "Cancer is very personal and what works for one person may not work for someone else." He told me not to get "bogged down with statistics." When I left, he walked me out and saw Bruce in the waiting room. He waved to him and asked him how he was doing.

Wednesday, 10/25:

Bruce and I went to the Cancer Center for his blood work and an appointment with P.A., Dee. Bruce's blood work was fine but his cancer markers are up from 387 to 668. We were both surprised since his Pet scan was so good. Dee spoke to Dr. Al and he said that since the Pet scan was recent, then that's what we have to go by and he's not changing anything with Bruce's treatment. We won't know anything for sure till the next set of scans—probably in January. Again, this is a real roller coaster.

Friday, 10/27-Saturday, 10/28:

Bruce and I spent two beautiful days at Cape May. We walked on the beach, had our meals out at different restaurants, prayed at a beautiful church, and shopped at the Cape May Mall. It was our first "vacation" in a long time and sadly, we had to cut it short. A terrible storm was predicted for Sunday, 10/29, so left for home late on Saturday.

Wednesday, 11/1:

Bruce had an appointment with Kay this morning and then chemo #2 of this cycle (14 total). His blood work was fine and he did well with chemo. He felt well afterwards and even ate dinner, which is unusual on chemo days.

Thursday, 11/2:

Bruce threw up during the night and this morning but still says he feels okay. No matter what he goes through, Bruce always remains positive. Not once has he felt sorry for himself or asked, "Why me?" If anything, he seems to think that there's a "bigger reason" why he's going through this.

Friday, 11/3:

Bruce had his chemo pump removed this afternoon and then did the meditation class. Once again, he had a great session—he saw a vision of a heart with all the vessels and he heard it beating. He also felt his body going upwards. I wish I could explain this but I don't understand it myself. Bruce just accepts it.

Saturday, 11/4:

This morning we went to Colin's last soccer game of the season. After we got home, Marc came up to interview us for his podcast. He was here a couple of hours and it went very well! Bruce, as always, enjoyed telling his "story."

Wednesday, 11/8:

Bruce had blood work and an appointment with Dr. Al this afternoon. Dr. Al said that unless Bruce's tumor markers continue to go up or if Bruce has specific symptoms, then he'll still wait till after chemo #6 to do the next set of scans.

Sunday, 11/12:

Purple Stride Day! It was held in Parsippany and almost 3,000 people came out to support pancreatic cancer. Team Hopatcong Hills was twice as big as last year and we raised twice the money we raised last year! Ken Rosato, from ABC News, was the host. Bruce and I got to talk to him prior to the opening ceremony. The survivors were on stage and some of them spoke. Bruce spoke and, as always, his words came from his heart. After the opening ceremony, we did the 5K. After Purple Stride, we hosted our second "Purple Luncheon" at Hopatcong's Northwood Fire House. Once again, Bruce spoke to our team after lunch. There are always some tears from different people whenever Bruce talks about his cancer journey.

Wednesday, 11/15:

Bruce and I went to chemo this morning. It went well and Bruce wasn't even sick afterwards. He did Yoga Nidra during chemo. He saw shiny white lights and other colors. I looked up white lights and it says it's your angels, particularly your guardian angel coming through. Bruce's meditation experiences are beyond anything I can understand or explain.

Thursday, 11/16:

World Pancreatic Cancer Day!

Friday, 11/17:

Bruce had his chemo pump removed today. We don't go back til the week after next.

Thursday, 11/23:

Happy Thanksgiving! Happy First Birthday, Ella Mae!

Carol, Doug, Michael and Laura and the boys, Debbie, Michael and the girls were all here for dinner. Chris and Jen and the kids came over after dinner and had dessert with us. The birthday girl looked like the little princess she is! I'm grateful to be able to celebrate another Thanksgiving with my family. I'm especially grateful that Bruce has also made it to enjoy another Thanksgiving and another family dinner and get-together.

Sunday, 11/26:

Today we attended the first brunch for Dylan's Rock on Foundation. Several people commented on how well Bruce looked. Bruce is a real "people person" and thrives on events such as this.

Wednesday, 11/29:

Bruce had an early appointment at the Cancer Center. We met with Kay who gave us disturbing news—Bruce's tumor markers are up again— the second time they've gone up and they've nearly doubled again. They went from 668 to 1,027! Kay said that now Dr. Al wants Bruce to have scans in December rather than wait til January as planned. This was definitely not the news we'd wanted to hear. As always, Bruce handled it much better than I did. He said as long as he feels good he's not going to worry about the markers. So now both of us will have Cat scans and doctor appointments before Christmas. It's been four years since we've had a Christmas without a "dark cloud" hanging over us.

Bruce did well with chemo during and after treatment. In the evening, he said that "Life is like a roller coaster with lots of ups and downs and that's how cancer markers are." Then he said that life would be boring without the ups and downs. I could take a little boring!

Friday, 12/1:

Bruce had his chemo pump removed today.

Friday, 12/8:

Bruce had his Cat scans today. Now the waiting begins. Then it'll be my turn.

Sunday, 12/10:

I checked my phone a little before 5:00 a.m.and saw that I'd gotten an email with Bruce's Cat scan results. I went out into the dining room to read the email so I wouldn't disturb Bruce. My hands were shaking and my heart was pounding. The chest scan is fine. According to the pelvic scan, the abdominal mass has grown from 1.5 cm to 3 cm. Bruce is discouraged and doesn't think the chemo is working. I'm very upset. We won't know anything until Dr. Al calls or we meet with him on Wednesday.

Wednesday, 12/13:

Bruce had an appointment with Dr. Al this morning and then chemo. It's difficult to explain but Bruce's mass has decreased slightly. Dr. Al explained everything to us. For now, Bruce is considered stable. He will remain on the same chemo regimen for at least two months. If Bruce's margins go up again, he will have new scans at that point. Otherwise, he'll have scans after three months. He can't have stronger chemo because then, if things worsen down the line, there will be nothing left to try. Dr. Al wants us to go back to Dr. Marie to get her opinion so I'll make that appointment tomorrow. He recommended a special blood test that he told us about a while ago. They test your blood to see what the best chemo would be for that person. It's considered experimental so insurance won't pay for it. It costs $1,500. We're going to go ahead with it. You get to a point where you'll do anything that might help.

Friday, 12/15:

Bruce went to have his pump removed and then to the hospital to get copies of his scans. Yesterday, I made an appointment for Tuesday with Dr. Marie and she wants to see the most recent scans.

Tuesday, 12/19:

Bruce and I had an appointment with Dr. Marie today. She's the pancreatic cancer specialist in New York City whom we met with in April. She was very pleased with Bruce's progress. Despite the mass in Bruce's abdomen, she considers him to be stable. She said he's on the correct chemo and should continue with it. Bruce was hoping he could stop the pump but she said what Dr. Al said—that he needs it. She did give us the name of something Bruce can take after chemo to mitigate the symptoms he complains about the most (no appetite, nausea, light-headedness, no energy). She said vitamin D infusions were only showing promise with the chemo Bruce was on after his surgery—not the chemo he's on now. She's very pleased that Bruce works out, is active, and watches his diet. We told Dr. Marie about Bruce's blog and she wrote the name down. She's going to send me info on pancreatic cancer that we can use for the blog. Dr. Marie asked Bruce if she could take his blood to use in her research. Of course, Bruce was more than happy to contribute to her research. When we got up to leave, Dr. Marie said how happy it makes her to see Bruce doing so well.

She hugged both of us. Finally, Dr. Marie said she'll call Dr. Al to fill him in on our visit. She gave us the best Christmas gift ever—the gift of hope!

Wednesday, 12/20:

Bruce's went for his blood work today. He saw Dr. Al and told him a little about our appointment with Dr. Marie.

Sunday, 12/24:

Today we had another beautiful Christmas Eve at Chris and Jen's house. Carol, Bruce, and I went over together. Doug met us there. It's always so much fun giving the kids their gifts! The boys are always so excited!

Monday, 12/25:

Merry Christmas! After exchanging presents, Bruce, Carol, and I went to the Cemetery to "visit" the family. Then we went to Debbie and Michael's for dinner. The most special gift this Christmas was a beautiful little book that Gianna made for Bruce on the past two years with Purple Stride. She wrote something beautiful on the last page. Bruce loved it and said it was the "most special gift" he's gotten in a very long time!

Wednesday, 12/27:

Bruce and I had to be at the Cancer Center by 7:30 this morning. After blood work, we had an appointment with Dr. Al. He's very pleased with Bruce's progress and with what Dr. Marie had to say. He thought it was wonderful that Bruce agreed to donate blood for research. We told him about the blog and asked if he'd be willing to take a picture with Bruce or make a little video. Well he agreed to do both! He did a great job talking off the cuff for a couple of minutes. He really is a special person! As one of the chemo nurses said, he always goes the extra step to do whatever he can for his patients.

Friday, 12/29:

Bruce went to the Cancer Center to have his pump removed. That's it till 2018! Hopefully, it'll be a good year!

PART FOUR

2018: January through December

Wednesday, 1/3:

Bruce went for blood work and an appointment with one of the physician assistants. Everything's fine: a very good way to start the New Year!

Wednesday, 1/10:

Bruce had chemo today. They checked his blood and tested for his markers. His blood work is fine and he did well with chemo.

Thursday, 1/11:

Today is the second anniversary of Bruce's surgery. We've been through so much these past three years and we've always bounced back from adversity and made the most of it! I can't believe all we've gotten involved with since Bruce's surgery. Here's to another good year for both of us! On the negative side, Bruce did throw up shortly after midnight. I actually thought I was hearing thunder. If only.

Friday, 1/12:

Bruce went down to have his pump removed today. He hates wearing the pump and always looks forward to having it removed.

Wednesday, 1/17:

Bruce went for blood work by himself. He told me his markers are "around 900" (high) but that "everything's stable." I'm not sure how that can be with such high tumor markers but I'll find out next week when I go to the cancer center with him.

Wednesday, 1/24:

Bruce had chemo this morning. His blood work is, as always, perfect. But his tumor markers went up from 923 to 1,217 in two weeks time. They'll be checked again in February and if they go up again, Bruce will have scans in February rather than in March. The Physician Assistant said that Bruce's case is "rare" because he's doing so well despite a malignant, stage four mass in his stomach. Let's hope he continues to do well!

Friday, 1/26:

Bruce had his chemo pump removed this morning. Afterwards, he felt light-headed and couldn't eat much.

Wednesday, 1/31:

When Bruce went for blood work, Dr. Al stopped in and told him about a new pill that's working to reduce some tumors. He ordered it for Bruce and we picked it up this evening. It's considered experimental but the insurance company paid for all but $10 of it (It cost $400 for a one month supply.).

Wednesday, 2/14:

Bruce had chemo today. His white blood count was a little low so they gave him a shot for that. Bruce went around giving the nurses and female chemo patients Valentine hugs. They love him down there!

Thursday, 2/15:

Bruce was sick a couple of times during the night. Today he was "out of it" all day. It's so sad watching him go through this and not being able to help him. I hope he feels better tomorrow.

Friday, 2/16:

Bruce felt much better today. We went to have his pump removed. His tumor markers have gone up again—by 60 points. It's discouraging. We were both hoping they'd be down a little this time.

From the Cancer Center, we went to the Sussex County YMCA for the first of six workshops for cancer survivors and caregivers. Each session is an hour and a half. There are about 15 of us, all with different and equally sad stories.

Wednesday, 2/21:

Bruce had blood work today and we met with Dee, one of the physican assistants. She wants Bruce to have his scans the third week in March—same week as mine.

Friday, 2/23:

Laura, who was recently diagnosed with breast cancer, had her first chemo infusion today. Like Bruce, she's ready to "kick cancer's butt." I was happy to see that attitude in her! I'm NOT happy that cancer has once again hit our family.

Bruce and I went to our second program at the Y for cancer survivors and caregivers. The people are all lovely but with the saddest stories.

Tuesday, 2/27:

Bruce and I walked a mile and a half at the park this morning. This is nothing for Bruce as he walks further than that every day!

Wednesday, 2/28:

Bruce had chemo today. He was pretty good once we got home. We both are always grateful for chemo days that go as well as today's did!

Friday, 3/2:

Bruce drove to the Cancer Center in snow today. There was no way he was going to let the snow prevent him from going down there and having his pump removed!

Tuesday, 3/6:

Bruce went for blood work this morning and to Livingston to pick up barium for my next set of Cat scans. After that, he had to go to St. Clare's to pick up barium for his own set of scans. Crazy life!

Saturday, 3/10:

Bruce and I walked with our Wage Hope friends in the St. Patrick's Day Parade in Morristown. Bruce helped carry our Pancan banner. After the parade, Bruce, Doug, and I went out to lunch.

Sunday, 3/11:

Great news this morning! I got an email about Bruce's scans. If I read it correctly, his mass decreased by two mm and everything else is clear!

Wednesday, 3/14:

Bruce and I went to his appointment with Dr. Al this morning. For the most part, I read the scans correctly. Everything is clear except for the mass in Bruce's stomach and that decreased by two millimeters. It's not much but we'll take it! Dr. Al is going to keep Bruce on the same schedule and same chemo since it appears to be working. We're thrilled for two millimeters of good news!

Friday, 3/16:

Bruce and I went to a Cancer Center to volunteer this morning and then went to our own Cancer Center to have Bruce's pump removed. Bruce and I both love volunteering but Bruce truly thrives on it—he loves talking to other cancer patients about all he's been through and has survived. He's doing more good than he realizes!

Saturday, 3/17:

Bruce took me for my Cat scans this morning. From there we went to Morris Catholic High School for Doug's 5K for St. Patrick's Day. It was a lot of fun and Doug did very well! A coach asked Bruce to hold down the flag (from the wind) at the start of the race so he even got involved!

A friend of mine sent me a message that he'd just completed treatment for prostate cancer. He said that Bruce and I "inspired" him in his own cancer diagnosis and treatments. He said (facetiously, of course) that all he had to do was say our names and he could "feel the cancer leaving" his body. I'm so blessed and grateful that Bruce and I have been able to do some good with the hands we've been dealt.

Tuesday, 3/20:

Today's health news is about myself: Bruce and I went to my appointment with Dr. Sam. My recent Can scan results showed that my kidney's fine and the nodule on my right lung is unchanged. The nodule on my left lung grew 1 millimeter, bringing it to 3 millimeters. Dr. Sam said it could be nothing but the report indicates that it could be a tumor or metastatic disease (worst case scenario). He's going to consult with a thoracic surgeon to see if she thinks the nodule should be monitored or require treatment.

Tuesday, 3/27:

Someone from Dr. Susan's office called me today. She's the thoracic surgeon Dr. Sam consulted with. She wanted me to go in next Wednesday to meet with her but I can't because Bruce has chemo then. So she's going to see if I can get an appointment on Monday. I'm hoping she just wants to talk to me and that this isn't something to be concerned about.

Wednesday, 3/28:

This was a wonderful evening! Bruce and I picked Doug up at 5:00 and we went to a local diner for dinner. Then we went to Doug's alma mater, Drew University, for a lecture by former Vice President Joe Biden. Doug got us VIP tickets and we were in the third row! Biden was great! After the program, Doug and I talked with Governor Tom Kean, who was Drew's President when Doug went there.

Monday, 4/2:

Despite a few inches of snow, Bruce and I made it to my appointment with the thoracic surgeon in Livingston. The news was disconcerting and unexpected. Dr. Susan said that the Pet scan I had a year ago showed a tiny nodule on my left lung. It's growing, is solid, and is one centimeter—three causes of concern. Dr. Susan already consulted with Dr. Sam and both agree that I need to have a Pet Scan. If that "lights up," I'll need to have a biopsy. If the biopsy is positive for cancer, I'd be operated on at that time. They'd remove the nodule and part of my lung surrounding it. If there's no lymph node involvement, it would be a stage one cancer. I'm so scared and overwhelmed. I can tell Bruce is scared too. Our family is going through so much and now this.

Tuesday, 4/3:

Bruce went to the support group in Morristown this evening. It was raining out but he wanted to go. I'm sure he needed it tonight.

Wednesday, 4/4:

Bruce and I met with Kay this morning. Bruce's white blood count was low again so he came home with a Neulasta patch. Chemo went well but the new pills (Which were to replace the chemo pump.) did not. Bruce was SO sick once we got home! He was light-headed and dizzy and threw up a lot. I felt so sorry for him.

Thursday, 4/5:

Bruce was sick all night and all day today. He threw up until 1:30 a.m. and again throughout the day. It had to be the chemo pills so we stopped them. The pump disperses the chemo gradually over a 48 hour period but the pills give you a big dose at once. Bruce was so sick he only ate a little applesauce all day and went to bed at 6:00 p.m.

Saturday, 4/7-Tuesday, 4/10:

Bruce and I spent a few days in Virginia with Michael, Laura, and the kids. I'm grateful Bruce is still healthy enough to drive five hours and then to play with the boys (They love climbing all over him!). Our visit was a nice distraction from all of our health issues.

Thursday, 4/12:

What a day! Very scary to start; huge relief at the end of it! Bruce took me for my Pet scan this morning. I was so scared and I could tell Bruce was too. He was so quiet. The test, from the dye injection and sitting for an hour, to drinking a bottle of warm barium (Ugh!) and sitting another 25 minutes, to the 25 minute scan took about two hours. The tech let me bring my prayer shawl into the room and he even placed it on top of me. That was very comforting. I mostly prayed and tried to meditate throughout the test. When we got home, there was a message from Dr. Susan asking me to call her about my test results. I assumed it was bad news since she called right away. I said to Bruce, "Well this can't be good." I was shaking as I called her. Dr. Susan got on and the news was good and bad. The good news is that the scan didn't light up so the nodule is unlikely to be cancerous. Dr. Susan put it at a 6% chance it's cancer. That was a HUGE relief! The bad news is that she thinks the nodule should be removed as it's been growing for a year, benign tumors can become malignant if left in the body too long, and there's a connection between kidney cancer and lung cancer. I had already decided I wanted to have the surgery even if it wasn't cancer. While I'm not looking forward to a second major surgery in three years (And my third major surgery.), I want this thing out of me. Dr. Susan said there's no emergency to removing it but that she wouldn't wait months. I told her about Pancreatic Cancer Advocacy Days in D.C. and she said there's no problem with waiting til after that—the last week in June. She'll be removing a piece of my lung in which the nodule is encased. If, God forbid, the biopsy does show cancer, then she'll remove more of my lung. Recovery is 6-8 weeks. Bruce and I are beyond grateful for this news; it could've been MUCH worse! Thank you, God!

Saturday, 4/14:

A long, exhausting, but worthwhile day! Bruce, Doug, and I went to New York Purple Stride at Prospect Park in Brooklyn with Pietrina and Anselmo. Bruce was on stage with the other survivors prior to the walk/run. He got to meet Barry, the founder of our NEGU group and to talk with him and his family. Camille, a stage 4 Pancreatic Cancer survivor, was there. A few others from our Wage Hope group were also there, including Franco, a pancreatic cancer survivor. This was another wonderful day to honor those with pancreatic cancer and those who have sadly lost their fight!

Thursday, 4/19:

Bruce had chemo yesterday and did much better with it this time than the last, when he was on the pills. He's back on the pump now. He was tired and just rested all day. Tomorrow, he'll have the pump removed.

Sunday, 4/22:

What an amazing day today was! Bruce and I left the house at 4:15 a.m. to pick Doug up, drive to Harrison, and then take the Path to the World Trade Center. We went to the 9/11 Memorial and Museum 5K. It was an emotional experience being there with thousands of people, including NYC Police and Fire Fighters. The course was around the Pier and NY police fleets went by blasting "America the Beautiful," "We Are the World," and other moving songs. I'm proud of all of us for doing this today! It was a day I won't forget!

Monday, 4/23:

I insisted that Bruce go to Urgent Care this morning as I didn't like the way the lump under his arm looked. The lump was an infected cyst. The doctor had to lance it, clean it, pack it, put a gauze bandage on it, put a gauze sling around it, and give Bruce an antibiotic. The doctor said had it broken open it could've infected his bloodstream!

Sunday, 4/29:

Bruce and I went to our second Purple Light. It was very emotional, especially when they showed our picture on a big screen, along with other survivors and several who've lost their battle with pancreatic cancer. I'm grateful Bruce is doing well but when I saw all those photos of people who have passed, it scared me so much!

Monday, 4/30:

Bruce took me to my check-up with Dr. Lee. He said my kidney function is good. He had read my Pet scan and said there doesn't appear to be any cancer but that we won't know for sure till a full biopsy is done. If this is cancer, then it's from the kidney cancer spreading.

Wednesday, 5/2:

This morning we met Debbie at Dr. Susan's office (On Debbie's birthday!). Dr. Susan explained the surgery. We scheduled it for June 26th. She'll make three small incisions, insert a camera, and remove the nodule and the piece of lung it's encapsulated in. Then they'll send it to pathology. Recuperation is 6 to 8 weeks. Here we go again!

After that appointment, we went to my appointment with Dr. Sam. He totally agrees with the surgery. He said since this nodule has been growing for a year and since there's a connection between kidney cancer and lung cancer, it has to come out. He said you can have a negative Pet scan (As I did.) and still have a malignancy. We won't know for sure till we get the full biopsy report back. He said if it is cancer it should be able to be treated since the nodule is so small. He cancelled my next Cat scan and appointment with him and told me to call three months after my surgery to reschedule. He wished me luck a couple of times.

Thursday, 5/3:

Bruce and I met Doug for dinner this evening and then we followed him to his school. We attended Sage's Art and Music Show, which was fantastic! Doug did a rap that he'd written with some of his students. He did a great job! I'm so glad we went to this program! I'm so proud of Doug and all of the students!

Monday, 5/7:

Bruce had an appointment with Kay and then chemo. Everything is good except that Bruce's white blood count was low again. They gave him Neulasta for that. After we got home, Bruce vomited a few times. He doesn't complain but I hate that he has to go through this. However, I'm grateful the chemo seems to be working.

Wednesday, 5/9:

Bruce had his chemo pump removed today. He felt much better after that.

Saturday, 5/12:

Today we went to Dylan's sixth Dinosaur Stomp. It was held at the firehouse due to rain. After Bruce took me home, he decided to go back to the firehouse. After he and Doug came home, Doug told me that Bruce gave an impromptu speech and that it was his "best speech yet." I was so sorry I missed it!

Tuesday, 5/15:

Happy Birthday, Bruce (#65) and many more!!! Doug did a birthday tribute to Bruce on our blog. Bruce had tears in his eyes listening to Doug's beautiful words. He said it was the "best birthday gift" he'd ever received!

What a beautiful tribute from a stepson to his stepfather. I'm so grateful for the bond Douglas has with Bruce.

Wednesday, 5/16:

Bruce and I went to his appointment with Dr. Al—in a terrible rainstorm. Our appointment went well. Bruce's next Cat scan will be the second week in June.

Despite the storm, we stopped for dinner and then went to our Wage Hope meeting. Bruce looks forward to these meetings and seeing everyone—even if the weather is miserable!

Monday, 5/21:

Bruce had chemo this morning. He was fine afterwards, which is always reason to give thanks.

Wednesday, 5/23:

Bruce and I went to the Cancer Center to have his pump removed. Starting with his next chemo, they're going to begin giving Bruce his anti-nausea medication through i.v. It's covered by insurance and should help Bruce more than the pills.

Thursday, 5/24:

Bruce and I went to a Pancan luncheon/meeting in Montville. It was a very nice gathering and also was very informative. Lisa, from our Wage Hope group, was there. She offered to go with Bruce to chemo the day after my surgery. Lisa's a four year pancreatic cancer survivor so it'll be really good for her to be there. It will certainly set my mind at ease.

Tuesday, 5/29:

Bruce went to the hospital to register for his scan tomorrow and to pick up his barium. Then he went to the Cancer Center for blood work and an appointment with one of the P.A.s. He has another boil under his arm so he showed the P.A. She agreed that he needs to have it lanced. He can't do that til after his Cat scan because he has to be able to put his arms above his head for the scan. We'll go to Urgent Care after Bruce's Cat scan.

Wednesday, 5/30:

Bruce and I went for his Cat scan. Now we do what we always do—wait for the results. Since Bruce looks and feels so good, I'm cautiously optimistic! From the hospital, we went for lunch and then to Urgent Care. Bruce had that nodule under his arm removed. It had to be numbed and lanced. Bruce said it was so painful because the doctor had to go in deep to remove it all. Now it'll be biopsied. Bruce is on an antibiotic and goes back on Saturday to have the stitches removed. So now we wait for Cat scan results and biopsy results. This is our life!

Friday, 6/1:

This was not a good start to a new month. The hospital emailed me Bruce's Cat scan results. It indicated that there was a "slight increase" in the size of the abdominal mass. I was crushed and hated having to tell Bruce. He was initially discouraged but later was back to his "fighting" self. I texted Dr. Al and he later got back to me. The news wasn't good. He said that there was "some progression to Bruce's cancer" and that his tumor markers have doubled. I'm beyond upset and scared. Bruce claims he's just a "little scared" but that he's not giving up and that this is just a "another bump in the road." What an incredulous attitude he continues to have! Even Dr. Al said what a "fighter" Bruce is. Dr. Al's going to order a Pet scan so we'll know more after that. He's adding a new and stronger drug to Bruce's chemo infusion, which will start on Monday. Since Bruce looks and feels so good and is so active, I wasn't overly concerned about this particular Cat scan. And now this. Also, I was hoping not to have to go into major surgery having to worry about Bruce. Too late for that.

Saturday, 6/2:

Bruce went to Urgent Care to have his stitches removed. The biopsy isn't back but the doctor said everything looked good. There's still a bandage on the wound. Bruce has to put warm compresses and a new bandage on it for a few days.

Monday, 6/4:

We got a lot of beautiful responses to Bruce's latest blog post. Many said how "inspirational" Bruce is.

Bruce and I went to the Cancer Center for chemo but Dr. Al cancelled it. He wants to see the results of Bruce's Pet scan before starting any new chemo treatment.

Tuesday, 6/5:

Bruce went to the monthly cancer support group at the Cancer Center in Morristown. This group is for all cancers so I could go too but I think it's important for Bruce to have a support group where he can talk openly without me there.

Wednesday, 6/6:

Bruce and I arrived at the hospital at 7:45 a.m. and left at 9:30 after Bruce's Pet scan. Dr. Al called around 4:30. He said the Pet scan confirmed the Cat scan—Bruce's abdominal mass has grown slightly but is confined to that one area. This means that the chemo Bruce has been on is no longer effective, something Dr. Al cautioned us about over a year ago. Bruce will begin the new chemo regimen on Monday. Dr. Al is going to look into immunology too. I asked about going to Dr. Marie and he agreed we should do that. So after we hung up, I called her office and scheduled an appointment for next Thursday. Doug has a half day that day and is going to take off so he can come with us. Doug came to our first appointment with Dr. Marie and was a big help. Bruce and I are so grateful he's agreed to do this for us again.

Thursday, 6/7:

Bruce went to the hospital to pick up his Cat and Pet scan discs. They included the report which mentioned that "the disease had spread." Dr. Al had already told me that but it's another thing to read it in black and white. This is SO scary!

Saturday, 6/9:

Bruce and Doug went to a PanCan 5K in Edison. Bruce even spoke at the event. Nothing discourages him or stops him!

Monday, 6/11:

Bruce went to Urgent Care this morning—his one ear was clogged and needed to be drained. Then he went to chemo by himself since I had Piper at the house. Bruce started on the new chemo and also had the anti-nausea meds given through i.v. Bruce did much better getting his anti-nausea meds this way. He wasn't nauseous during or after chemo. He came home like it was any other day—he was himself, his face wasn't reddish, he never threw up, and he ate dinner! I was worried about him going alone but he did fine. Now I hope the new chemo shrinks his tumor.

Thursday, 6/14:

Bruce, Doug, and I went to Bruce's appointment with Dr. Marie. It went better than expected. Despite the fact that Bruce's abdominal mass has grown, she said it's very good news that it hasn't spread. She agrees with the new chemo cocktail Dr. Al put Bruce on. As for the high tumor markers (CA 19), Dr. Marie said: "I treat people, not numbers." I loved that statement and so did Bruce and Doug. However, Dr. Marie will continue to monitor those markers and wants to see the next set. She also wants to see Bruce's next Cat scan. She said that even if this new chemo doesn't work, there are several other things we can do. I found that very encouraging. Bruce asked about exercising. She said to continue to do it as it's very important. I asked about diet. She said the one thing to avoid is sugar, which we already knew.

Friday, 6/15:

Bruce took me for my pre-admission blood work. Then we went to the Cancer Center for Bruce's blood work. I told the physician assistant about our appointment with Dr. Marie. She's going to fax over Bruce's Foundation Medicine results to Dr. Marie (Nothing showed up that would be a target for cancer.).

Sunday, 6/17-Tuesday, 6/19:

Pancreatic Cancer Advocacy Days—our second one and it was as amazing as last year! I'm so glad, given our health issues, that Bruce and I were able to attend and participate again this year! The most exciting part was that we got to meet with Senator Cory Booker in his office on Capitol Hill. He was wonderful! He spoke to each of us individually. He really seemed interested in our stories. He spent a lot of time with us and took pictures afterwards. Of course, Bruce managed to stand right next to Senator Booker for the pictures!

Tuesday, 6/19-Sunday, 6/24:

Bruce and I drove to Michael and Laura's after we returned to the hotel from Capitol Hill. We enjoyed spending time with them and the kids!

Tuesday, 6/26:

Bruce and I got to the hospital by 6:00 a.m. My surgery started around 7:15. Dr. Susan removed the nodule with the portion of the lung that surrounded it. Then it was sent to pathology. We went into this knowing I had only a 6% chance of this being cancerous. Well, wouldn't you know, I'm in the 6%. The nodule tested positive for renal cancer. Dr. Susan said she was shocked. She already called Dr. Sam. I have two nodules on my right lung so they're already talking about removing those and then doing chemo. After three and a half years of being cancer free, I thought I was going to beat this. I guess cancer had other ideas. The family and I are devastated.

Wednesday, 6/27:

I received several messages of support after Chris' two FaceBook posts about me. He did a beautiful job, as he's done in the past. Dr. Susan said again how surprised she was that the nodule was cancerous. I have to go see her in two weeks and then have a Cat scan. Then a decision will be made about a second surgery and then chemo. I can't believe this is happening. I was discharged this evening—late but at least I got to go home.

Monday, 7/2:

Debbie spoke with Dr. Sam's nurse about me this morning. She told Debbie that Dr. Sam is under the impression that I will have the second surgery and then he'll discuss chemo with me. I'm still having problems processing all of this. If Bruce and I both need chemo, then we have no life to speak of. And I don't want to live like that. I'm more interested in the quality of life than the quantity. I want to live a long life but I don't want to agree to chemo unless Dr. Sam can tell me he's pretty sure it will help to prolong my life. I can't believe I'm in this situation.

Friday, 7/6:

Bruce left the house at 5:00 a.m. to meet Ann Marie in Little Falls. He went into the City with her for the ringing of the New York Stock Exchange bell! PANCAN was invited along with a pharmaceutical company that does research on pancreatic cancer. The "Core Team" of our Wage Hope group was invited.

Monday, 7/9:

Bruce had chemo today. A friend picked him up, drove him there, and stayed with him throughout chemo.

Wednesday, 7/11:

Today was my first day out of the house in two weeks! Bruce took me to the hospital for chest x-rays.Then we went to my appointment with Dr. Susan. She said my x-rays were fine and that my left lung is fully inflated. My incisions are healing nicely and I'm recovering "remarkably well" for being just two weeks out of surgery. The biopsy showed what the initial one did—the nodule she removed was positive for renal cancer. Thankfully, the margins were clear! Dr. Susan said that even if the nodule on my right lung hasn't changed, it'll still have to come out since the other one was cancerous. So it looks like I'll be having another surgery at the end of August. From Dr. Susan's, we went to the Cancer Center so Bruce could have his chemo pump removed.

Saturday, 7/14:

Bruce, Chris, Doug, Sean, Jake, and Colin all went to a Red Bulls' game this evening. This was Bruce's first pro soccer game and it was on his "Bucket List." I'm so glad Chris invited Bruce to go with them. He had a wonderful time!

Monday, 7/16:

Bruce had an appointment with Dr. Al plus blood work. Bruce's blood work was fine but his tumor markers are still very high. Dr. Al said Bruce is "highly unusual" in how he's progressed with this disease and with how well he's handled chemo. I gave Dr. Al a copy of my pathology report and filled him in on things. He said renal cancer is tricky because it travels through the blood and can come on suddenly and appear anywhere. He said it's good that the markers on the left lung are clear but that the nodule on the right lung has to be removed. He said chemo won't help because there's no way to pinpoint a location for it as there is with other cancers. He said there are meds that would help. He told me to make an appointment with him after I recover from my next surgery.

Wednesday, 7/18:

Bruce went to a Wage Hope meeting this evening. I skipped the meeting. Whenever I don't go, Bruce enjoys going down earlier to help set up and staying later to help cleanup (And talk!).

Thursday, 7/19:

Bruce and I had a very relaxing day today! We decided to go to Round Valley State Park in Clinton. We sat by the Lake, watched the kids swimming, had lunch there, talked, and even just sat in silence. Going to the Park was a spur of the moment decision that turned out to be a very good one!

Monday, 7/23:

Bruce had chemo today. I'm still in some pain and didn't think I could sit there all those hours so he went by himself. Bruce said he'd be fine going alone and he was. You'd never know he had chemo with this new regimen. Thank you, God!

Wednesday, 7/25:

Bruce had his pump removed today. He continues to do very well with this chemo. I'm also doing well—I walked three miles on my treadmill today (One mile at a time but I did it!).

Thursday, 7/26:

Laura's surgery was today—they got the mass and there was no cancer in her lymph glands! Such a huge relief!

Monday, 7/30:

Bruce, Doug, and I went into the City today. We had a very long walk to the Circle Line, which we took for the third time. It's a two and a half hour trip. The weather was perfect. After our "cruise," we walked back and had dinner before heading over to Port Authority and back home. Fun days like this are a welcome respite from all of our medical days. Bruce and I were both grateful to Doug for organizing this "outing" to the City!

Tuesday, 7/31:

Bruce went for blood work and the news wasn't good. A physician assistant called to tell me that Bruce's hemoglobin was low. He has to have it rechecked on Friday.

Thursday, 8/2:

Great news: Laura went to the doctor and learned that she's cancer free! I'm overjoyed! My prayers have been answered!

Bruce and I went to the Seniors' meeting this morning. Odin, a beautiful four year old St. Bernard was there. Odin has bone cancer and his owners bring him to various meetings and events. He only has a few months to live. Bruce and I got to meet Odin's owners prior to the meeting. Of course, Bruce sat on the floor and petted and played with Odin.

Friday, 8/3:

I went with Bruce for his blood work and appointment with P.A. Barbara. Thankfully, Bruce's hemoglobin is back to normal. Barbara was afraid Bruce might have been bleeding somewhere. She still thinks it's a good idea to go to the gastro specialist.

Saturday, 8/4:

This morning, I had my Cat scans done. If it's not Bruce, it's me! At least we're in sync!

Monday, 8/6:

Bruce had chemo today and I was able to join him for the first time in over a month. Bruce's blood work is fine. Dr. Al wants Bruce to have a Cat scan the end of August. Bruce did well with chemo today.

Tuesday, 8/7:

Sadly, Odin passed away this morning. We just met him and now he's gone. His owners had a memorial at the Sussex Airport which Bruce went to. I passed on it as the weather was terrible (thunderstorms). Bruce told me later they had tents set up. Still, I was worried about him catching a cold or worse out there.

Wednesday, 8/8:

I had an appointment with Dr. Sam today. He said that the scans show that my left lung is still clear. Good news there! The nodule on my right lung hasn't changed or grown. More good news! Dr. Sam said because that nodule hasn't grown, it's probably benign. But after what happened on the left side, he won't totally commit to that. He said that since my cancer spread to my lung, I have metastatic renal cancer. Not good news but I'd already suspected that.

Monday, 8/13:

Bruce had blood work today. It was perfect, including his hemoglobin.

Wednesday, 8/15:

I had an appointment with Dr. Susan this morning. She said that while the nodule on my right lung appears to be benign, it could always be like the other one—malignant renal cancer. Worst case scenario: lung cancer. In that case, Dr. Susan would remove the lower lobe of my lung. I'm not even going to "go there." Surgery is scheduled for September fourth.

Friday, 8/17:

Bruce had an appointment with Dr. Dean, our new gastro doctor. The doctor said Bruce doesn't need a colonoscopy. He doesn't want to "jump the gun" on an endoscopy since Bruce's blood work is better now. He said it's not unusual to become anemic after a Whipple. The doctor told us that his uncle died from pancreatic cancer so of course we talked about that. Bruce gave him one of our business cards. Dr. Dean said that sometimes people "just need a little hope." Despite everything he's dealing with I don't know anyone better at offering hope to those who need it than Bruce.

Monday, 8/20:

Bruce had chemo this morning. I didn't go since our Virginians were here. Bruce met with Dr. Al, who told him that his markers have gone up a few hundred points—over 3,000 now. Naturally, this is very upsetting. We won't know anything until after Bruce's next Cat scan.

Tuesday, 8/21:

Bruce secretly made a video for the blog for my birthday, which is today. He had Doug tape it outside this past Sunday. It's four minutes of Bruce praising me and saying how much he loves me. It was so very sweet—something I'll treasure forever.

Wednesday, 8/22:

Bruce had his chemo pump removed today. I still can't get over that beautiful video Bruce made for me—such a special birthday gift.

Sunday, 8/26:

Bruce and I met Doug for breakfast and then we followed him to his new church in Parsippany. There was a live band that played and sang for fifteen minutes. Then there was the sermon, which was about a true story—about a movie that starred Dennis Quaid—"Imagine this." Quaid plays a father who's dying from pancreatic cancer. It was so moving. Bruce had tears in his eyes the entire time. Doug wanted us to be there when he heard what the subject of today's sermon would be. After the service, Bruce said he'd gotten more out of this service than any other in his life. I'm glad it had such a profound effect on him. In the lobby, Bruce spoke to the Pastor, told him his story, gave him one of our business cards, and even offered to speak on stage. One sermon and Bruce is ready to replace the Pastor!

Monday, 8/27:

Bruce had his Cat scans this morning. Since his tumor markers are so high, I'm quite concerned about these scans.

Wednesday, 8/29:

Bruce's results were emailed to me and I read them early this morning. They indicate a progression in his abdominal mass. I was beyond upset to learn this. When I told Bruce, he was quiet at first but then handled it better than I did (As per usual.). We had an appointment with Dr. Al in the afternoon. He said the bad news is that the mass has grown. The good news is that it hasn't spread. Chemo is no longer working so that's suspended til further notice. He wondered if the mass could be removed so he called Dr. Marie for advice. She said it's a rare surgery but might be possible. Next, Dr. Al texted a pancreatic cancer surgeon in the City. This doctor said resecting the mass is definitely an option. Dr. Al gave me this doctor's info. I spent our entire car ride going home on the phone with his staff. Bruce has an appointment for a consultation on September 12th. It's only a week past my next surgery but I'm hoping to be able to go with Bruce to the appointment. It's too important for me to miss. God help us as we move forward with our cancer journeys.

Thursday, 8/30:

Bruce and I went to the hospital to have Bruce's pathology reports sent to the surgeon we're going to see on September 12th. Being back in that hospital brought memories of Bruce's Whipple.

Monday, 9/3:

Bruce, Doug, and I went to Lake Mohawk's Labor Day 5K today. Doug ran; Bruce and I walked. This 5K was Bruce's eighth and my sixth. And I'm having major surgery tomorrow!

Tuesday, 9/4:

We got to the hospital at 6:00 a.m. Chris came while I was in pre-op. Surgery was more complicated than the last one because of scar tissue, inflammation, and grittiness on the lung which had to be scrapped. This was from my chest surgery thirty years ago. But the good news is that the nodule was benign! Thank God!

Wednesday, 9/5:

Dr. Susan and a few residents came in this morning. She explained the surgery to me and how complicated it was. Because of all the scrapping she had to do plus having to lift that lung away from the rib cage, plus cutting and removing the nodule and surrounding piece of lung has resulted in a lot more pain than my previous lung surgery. Bruce was here most of the day. God bless him!

Friday, 9/7:

Bruce stayed with me all day today. My main nurse lost her father to pancreatic cancer. She, Bruce, and I talked about her loss as well as Bruce's fight with pancreatic cancer. The food service man delivered my dinner a little early as he'd heard I was going to be released. He told me "everyone" loves me and that "they're not going to let" me leave. I guess that means I'm a good patient! It's not hard to be nice to the wonderful staff at this hospital! I was released from the hospital later on in the evening—the staff lined up in the hall to say goodbye and wish me luck.

Sunday, 9/9:

A very scary morning. Last night, I noticed that my bandages were moist. I just figured I'd spilled a little water on them. But this morning, it was worse—they were all wet. I had Bruce look at them and he said they were bleeding. I called Dr. Susan's office at 7:30 a.m. and she returned my call ten minutes later. She told me to have Bruce remove the bandages, which he did. She said if the blood was bright red I'd have to go to the E.R. If it was yellow or light pink, it was okay. I was so scared! Thankfully, it was a yellowish color. Dr. Susan said this was fluid oozing from my chest and nothing to worry about. She said to blot the area and put a big bandage on it, which we did. I'm so grateful it wasn't anything worse!

Wednesday, 9/12:

Bruce and I went into the City for Bruce's appointment with Dr. B. The doctor was very pleased with how well Bruce is doing—that he looks and feels fine; that he's eating; and that he's very active. He said all those things are very important. He did blood work and ordered a Cat scan for Friday. After he gets those results, he'll call us. Then a decision will be made about whether or not the mass can be removed. If it can't, Dr. B said there are other chemo options. So that was our bit of encouragement for today—and also what I had prayed for. We got home around 5:30. I was in terrible pain and went to bed with a heating pad. Bruce went to a Wage Hope meeting.

Thursday, 9/13:

I was in a lot of pain all day—I'm sure it was from being out all day yesterday. Bruce went to the hospital to sign for the pathology labs the New York doctor needs to move forward.

Friday, 9/14:

Bruce went for his scans this morning. I wish I could've gone with him but I was in too much pain. He said they did three scans: chest, pelvis, and liver.

Tuesday, 9/18:

Dr. B called and we talked with him for a long time. Bruce's new x-rays showed the abdominal mass that we knew about. But it also showed a few spots within Bruce's abdomen that did not show up on the previous scans. Surgery is no longer an option. Dr. B spoke with Dr. Al and they agree that the next step is to get Bruce on a clinical trial. Dr. B set up an appointment for Bruce with a pancreatic cancer oncologist in the City. He also wants me to make an appointment with Dr. Marie to get her advice. Dr. B said he, Dr. Al, and Dr. Marie will work together to decide on the best plan for Bruce. The doctor said not to underestimate the fact that Bruce continues to look and feel good. He said sometimes that tells more about what's going on than the scans do. Dr. B said he's confident that Bruce can reach the three year mark in January and beyond. I sure hope so! As always, Bruce's attitude throughout this was amazing! He's "excited" that there's something else out there for the doctors to try and is optimistic that it will work. I'm sure Bruce's positive attitude from day one has helped him to get this far and do this well.

Wednesday, 9/19:

I called Dr. Marie's office and made an appointment for Bruce for October second. I have Dr. Al next Wednesday, Bruce has Dr. Ann next Friday, and Bruce has Dr. Marie the following Tuesday. I feel like we're on a merry-go-round that just won't stop.

Friday, 9/21:

I called PanCan in California today. I put the rep on speaker so Bruce and I could both talk with her. She gave us a lot of info on clinical trials and answered all of our questions. Later, she emailed me several pages of info to read and discuss with the two specialists we're going to next Friday and the following Tuesday.

Saturday, 9/22:

Bruce went to Urgent Care after the gym this afternoon. He has a small scab on top of his head that's been bothering him. I told him it was probably a bug bite. Boy was I wrong! Turns out he has Shingles! I couldn't believe it! He has scabs on his head and smaller ones on his chin, neck, and behind one ear. He's on two medications and a cream. I'm so afraid this might interfere with clinical trials. I'm praying Bruce has a mild case.

Monday, 9/24:

Bruce and I went to see Dr. Adam this afternoon. I wanted him to check Bruce because of the Shingles. He said that Bruce has a mild case and should be fine. Thank Goodness!

Tuesday, 9/25:

Today's entry is all about Chris! Jen took him to Hackettstown' s E.R. due to severe abdominal pain and a high white blood count. Bruce and I went to the hospital in the afternoon. A Cat scan showed that Chris had appendicitis and needed emergency surgery. The surgeon said if Chris didn't have the surgery, he'd die! After they whisked Chris to the O.R., Bruce, Jen, and I went to the cafeteria to get something to eat and to wait for the doctor to come out. While we were waiting, Dr. Al called to ask how Bruce was doing. Back to Chris—the surgeon came out and said he removed Chris' appendix, which was enlarged and inflamed. The doctor said Chris will probably be released tomorrow. Prior to Chris' surgery, the doctor noticed the scabs on Bruce's face and asked what it was. He seemed surprised when we told him it was the Shingles. He said he feared it could be Melanoma. Then we told him that Bruce is a pancreatic cancer survivor. He seemed shocked that Bruce appeared to be fine except for his Shingles. Thank God this day is over and that Chris will be alright!

Wednesday, 9/26:

Bruce took me to my first appointment with Dr. Al. He told me what I already knew—that my diagnosis is stage four metastatic renal cancer (Since the cancer went to my lung.). He's going to continue with three months' scans. Of course, we also talked about Bruce. Dr. Al's looking into clinical trials as Bruce and I are also doing.

Friday, 9/28:

Today was Bruce's appointment with Dr. Ann. We were there about three hours. Here are the highlights: There are trials and immunology therapies but there's a waiting list. Bruce signed the forms to be placed on these lists. Once they come to him, Bruce would still have to be approved. It's very discouraging. I just want to move forward now, not wait. Dr. Ann took Bruce's blood for more detailed gene testing than he had before. She thinks Bruce should go back on the original chemo he was on until a spot for a trial opens up for him. She's going to call Dr. Al to explain everything to him. Dr. Ann gave us the names of two cancer centers in Philadelphia that she wants us to look into for clinical trials. She also suggested we look into trials in New Jersey.

Tuesday, 10/2:

Today we had our appointment with Dr. Marie. She spoke with Dr. Al and they've agreed on a new chemo regimen if Bruce doesn't get into a clinical trial or if there's a long wait before he does. She recommended a trial at Weil Cornell's kidney foundation, the Rogosin Institute. She called over there and got us an appointment. We met one of the doctors in charge and she explained the trial to us. It's a "macro bead" trial. Eight tiny beads containing cells of mice with kidney cancer would be surgically implanted into Bruce's stomach. Kidney cancer tricks the immune system into thinking it has kidney cancer rather than pancreatic cancer and thereby activates the immune system. This therapy has mainly been used for colon cancer patients—and it has proven to be successful. It's now in phase four of the trial for colon cancer. Because colon cancer and pancreatic cancer act the same regarding the immune system, they decided to try it with pancreatic cancer patients. They're only in the second phase so there are no guarantees. The doctor said that Bruce would go into the hospital one day for Cat and Pet scans and another day to have the beads implanted. Once they have and review Bruce's medical records, they'll call us with a decision. (Too bad I couldn't have given Bruce my cancerous kidney cells!)

Wednesday, 10/3:

Bruce went to the hospital to have his scan reports and discs sent to the Institute in the City. I wish all medical reports and scans could be in one place digitally so that they could automatically be sent over to various doctors and hospitals. Bruce has already spent a lot of time picking up his medical records in order to bring them to all of these different doctors and locations.

Thursday, 10/4:

This was a draining day and it's really beginning to get to me. Dr. N called. She and her team don't think the bead trial would benefit Bruce. She suggested we go with a trial at Sloan. I was very disappointed. I called Sloan and left a message with someone. Then I called Dr. Marie's office and left a message with someone there. Dr. Marie called back. She's going to call the Institute to find out why Bruce was turned down. After Dr. Marie called, Ruth from MSK called. She talked for almost a half hour about a brand new trial (phase 1) that just opened up. Only nine sites nation-wide are offering it and only twenty patients will be accepted at MSK. It would require a huge commitment—hours on end several days a week for the first 28 days. Since it's only phase one, there are no completed case studies. Bruce would essentially be a "guinea pig."

Besides fielding phone calls, Bruce and I went to the Seniors' meeting. He spoke about pancreatic cancer and Purple Stride. He did a very good job!

Friday, 10/5:

After worrying about all that was involved with the MSK trial, Ruth called today to say that Dr. V said there are no openings at this time. They will keep Bruce on their waiting list. I texted Dr. Al to tell him what's going on. He texted Dr. Marie and then got back to me. Dr. Marie told him that there are no openings on the Weil Cornell trial. She told Dr. Al she wants Bruce back on chemo as soon as possible. Dr. Al arranged for Bruce to begin next Wednesday. After this, the head nurse from the Cancer

Center called to give us our appointment. She said she was sorry the trials didn't work out but that the good news was that they'd all get to see us. I'll research other clinical trials beginning on Monday.

This was a sad day for the family. Michael and Laura had to put Jeter down this afternoon. Jeter had cancer and the Vet said it was time. Bruce and I spent a lot of time with Jeter over the years and will miss him.

Tuesday, 10/9:

One of the women I called at Hackensack's Cancer Center yesterday returned my call. She asked a lot of questions of Bruce and me. She made us an appointment for October 25th. This is in regard to clinical trials. It would be wonderful if Bruce got accepted into a trial at Hackensack.

This evening, on our way to a concert in Morristown, Bruce told me that he's been having pains in his stomach the past few days. He said they're not severe, that they go away when he walks, and that they come and go. Since his mass is in his abdomen, I'm truly a nervous wreck! I'm not sleeping and I always have a heaviness in my chest and stomach. I'm the one doing all the paperwork and I have a lot of forms that were sent from Hackensack that I have to fill out. I think I've handled everything quite well since my own diagnosis but it's all getting to me now. (Needless to say, I didn't enjoy the concert once Bruce told me about the pains in his stomach.)

Wednesday, 10/10:

I've been awake since 3:00 a.m. I'm so worried about Bruce. The stress is beginning to overwhelm me.

Bruce resumed chemo today after having over a month off of it. He started a new kind, which Dr. Marie recommended: MIC. It'll be two weeks on and two weeks off. I'm praying it works.

Friday, 10/12:

Bruce did water therapy for the first time. It was a gift from Doug. Bruce loved it! He found it very relaxing and peaceful.

Saturday, 10/13:

Bruce still has that pain in his side. He said it hurts most when he bends over. He told me he wants me to call Dr. Al on Monday and ask if he should have a Cat scan. I'm so scared.

Sunday, 10/14:

This morning, Bruce wished me a happy anniversary (#29). Then he said he thought he should get to the Emergency Room as his pain was worse. I totally panicked and had to take a Xanax. I texted Dr. Al and asked where we should go. He said to go to St. Clare's, since that's where Bruce's records were. I called and texted Chris and Jen to see if one of them could drive us but I didn't hear back right away so I called J.P. He was nice enough to drive us to the hospital. Chris texted in the meantime and said he was on his way to the hospital. JP stayed with me until Chris got there. I was so grateful Chris was there for both Bruce and for me. I was so nervous! The ER doctor did blood work and then a Cat scan. He called one of Dr. Al's associates and he came in to talk to us. He said there's only a slight change in Bruce's abdominal mass. But there is more fluid around the mass, which isn't a good thing. The doctor didn't think it was significant enough to hospitalize Bruce. He said to just keep our appointment with Dr. Al on Wednesday. I was so relieved. I was really afraid the mass had grown or was pressing against a nerve.

Monday, 10/15:

Bruce still has that pain. I wish they had drained the fluid while he was in the hospital.

Tuesday, 10/16:

Bruce and I met Doug for dinner to celebrate his birthday (Doug's). Thankfully, Bruce felt much better today and was able to enjoy dinner.

Wednesday, 10/17:

Bruce had an appointment with Dr. Al this afternoon and then chemo. Dr. Al said that the fluid the ER doctor told us about is minor and doesn't need to be drained. Bruce's pain is from cancerous tissue that's pressing against his abdominal mass. The mass has grown slightly and Bruce's tumor markers are up again. Dr. Al said that we're "running out of options"—very scary to hear. He said to continue to pursue clinical trials as they seem to be Bruce's best bet now. He told us about a 44 year old friend of his with three young kids who was recently diagnosed with pancreatic cancer. Of course, Bruce offered to talk with him and told Dr. Al to give him our number. In the chemo room, one of the nurses asked Bruce if he would talk to a breast cancer patient who was there. Bruce spent several minutes with her and clearly cheered her up. Before she left, she came over to thank Bruce for talking with her. Bruce continues to help and inspire people along their own cancer journeys. And he continues to believe he's going to beat this! I pray he's right!

Thursday, 10/18:

Despite chemo yesterday and the news we received from Dr. Al, Bruce felt fine all day today! As my mother would say, "God bless him!"

Sunday, 10/21:

Bruce and I did a Breast Cancer 5K in Parsippany today. We did this one for Laura. Later, we went to the boys' soccer games. We always enjoy watching the boys play!

Wednesday, 10/24:

Bruce went for blood work today and his white blood count was low. He has to go back Tuesday for follow-up blood work. Bruce's pain was a little worse today. He didn't look well to me and he went to bed around 5:00 to rest—very unusual for him. He got up about an hour later. I was so worried about him. I can't even put into words how I feel physically and emotionally. Unless you've gone through it as a patient and/or a caregiver, you just wouldn't understand.

Thursday, 10/25:

Bruce and I got to Hackensack's Cancer Center around 2:00. He had five vials of blood taken. His white blood count is still low. A woman took us up to the fourth floor for our appointment with Dr. G. He has a trial for Bruce and it opens up in a couple of weeks! We're thrilled! The doctor and his nurse explained everything and sent us home with lots of information to read, digest, and sign. This trial will mean no more chemo til further notice. Our next appointment is on November 6th—mainly an informational session. Now we pray that Bruce responds well to this trial and that it extends his life.

Friday, 10/26-Monday, 10/29:

Bruce and I spent the weekend in Virginia with Michael, Laura, and the kids. On Friday, I read to Dominic's pre-school class. On Saturday, Michael, Bruce, and all three kids and I went to the Air and Space Museum. On Sunday, we went to a farm. It was the first time Bruce went to a farm for Halloween and he really enjoyed it, especially being with the kids (Everything they did, he did!). This day was such a nice, pleasant break for both of us!

Tuesday, 10/30:

Bruce went to the Cancer Center for blood work. His white blood count was up a little, but still low. As for the pain, Bruce said it comes and goes. Extra Strength Tylenol seems to help. I just hate that it's there on a regular basis.

Wednesday, 10/31:

Bruce and I went to Jake and Colin's Halloween parade at school today. Ella was dressed as Minnie Mouse and looked adorable!

Bruce's pain really bothered him this evening. He's now taking Tylenol every day (And Bruce always hated taking medicine, even for a headache.). He said the pain is fine when he's working out or walking but that it's bad when he's sitting or lying down. He went to bed at 5:00 p.m. but did get up a couple hours later. I feel so badly for all he's going through. My heart's always heavy and I'm always looking at him for any changes and asking him how he's feeling. It also means my own health issues take a back seat. I was supposed to go for a second follow-up with Dr. Susan but I can't make the appointment because I never know when we'll be able to go due to Bruce's schedule and health. I've already cancelled two dentist appointments and two eye doctor appointments.

Friday, 11/2:

Bruce and I picked Doug up at his place and then headed to Philadelphia. After we checked into our hotel, we went for a walk and then to dinner. It was such a nice evening!

Saturday, 11/3:

Bruce, Doug, and I went to Philadelphia's Purple Stride this morning. Bruce was on stage with the other survivors. Afterwards, he got to talk with several of them. Then we all did the 5K. As always, Doug ran and Bruce and I walked. It was a very special day waging hope for pancreatic cancer!

Tuesday, 11/6:

Bruce had a short appointment at Hackensack's Cancer Center. His white blood count is still too low for him to begin a clinical trial. They've already chosen the trial for Bruce. He'll begin on November 26th if all goes well at our next appointment on Friday.

Wednesday, 11/7:

Bruce took me to my appointment with Dr. Lee this morning. Dr. Lee said he was surprised when he'd heard that the nodule on my left lung tested positive for renal cancer. He said since I'd been doing so well, he thought I was "out of the woods." I told him after three and a half years, I thought so too! He agrees that I don't need chemo meds as long as I'm cancer free. Bruce was in the room with me so we filled Dr. Lee in on what's been going on with him.

Thursday, 11/8:

The hospital called to schedule my Cat scans. I could've gone any time but I decided to go after Thanksgiving. Every November for the past four years, Bruce and I have gotten bad news. So just in case, I figured I'd hold off till after Thanksgiving.

Friday, 11/9:

Bruce and I went to Hackensack Hospital for an appointment with Dr. H. Thankfully, Bruce's white blood count went up so he can begin a clinical trial. They did more extensive blood work, gave Bruce three EKGs, and had him sign several consent forms. Then we had to schedule a Cat scan. The clinical trial Bruce will be on was selected specifically for him based on his markers, T cells, and immune system. The trial is new so there are no statistics for it. There are no guarantees but it's our best hope for now. As our NEGU group says: We Will Never Ever Give Up!

Saturday, 11/10:

Bruce and I set up the Hopatcong Northwood Firehouse for our third "Purple Luncheon," which is tomorrow. Afterwards, Bruce went down to Parsippany to pick up our Purple Stride shirts and help set up for tomorrow.

Sunday, 11/11:

Today was our third Purple Stride 5K for Pancreatic Cancer. We had another good team! Bruce was on stage with the other survivors for the opening ceremony. After that, we walked with around 3,000 people! From Purple Stride, we headed to the firehouse for our "Purple Luncheon." Bruce spoke to the group, as he also did last year and the year before that. He always talks from his heart and is always so sincere. Today was another successful and emotional Purple Stride and "Purple Luncheon"! God willing, we'll all be here next year to do it again—-especially Bruce!

Monday, 11/12:

Dr. V called about Bruce's genetic testing. There's no heredity factor to Bruce's cancer. There are three markers indicative of pancreatic cancer. Dr. V wished Bruce luck and said if, at any point, the trial stops working for him, to call her and she'll see what she can do to help him. That was encouraging to both of us.

Wednesday, 11/14:

Bruce and I went to Ambulatory Care to pick up my last three cat scan discs and reports. Then we went to Mt. Lakes to drop them off. We went in the back to see the nurses. They were as happy to see us as we were to see them! They're a very special group of dedicated nurses! From there we went to a diner for dinner and then to a Wage Hope meeting. So it was a busy and productive day!

Thursday, 11/15:

Today was World Pancreatic Cancer Day. Thanks to Bruce and our Mayor, it was recognized in Town with a sign by Town Hall and purple ribbons around trees in the park.

Friday, 11/16:

Bruce and I went to Hackensack for more blood work and a Cat scan. He had ten vials of blood taken in the infusion room. It was our first time in there and we were very impressed with the facilities and the nurses!

Saturday, 11/17:

Today we drove to Gordon's apartment and then the three of us went out to lunch. Gordon is from our Wage Hope group and is very special to Bruce and me. He lost his father and a close friend to pancreatic cancer. The three of us spent a very pleasant afternoon together! An added bonus for Bruce was getting to spend time with Gordon's dog, Buddy.

Sunday, 11/18:

This morning, we drove over an hour in order to attend a Never Ever Give Up Brunch. We got to talk with friends we'd met before and we also got to meet new friends. Although the stories were naturally sad, we all talked and laughed and had a great time! It's always good for Bruce to talk with other survivors.

Tuesday, 11/20:

I received a copy of Bruce's Cat scan results this morning. They showed what we were already aware of—a small mass in his abdomen and a cancerous mass of tissue pressing against it. This is what causes Bruce's pain. The Cat scan results mentioned something about fluid within the liver that is indicative of cancer. It wasn't there a month ago at Bruce's last scan. This is very disconcerting and upsetting to both of us.

After dinner, Bruce's pain came back so he took Extra Strength Tylenol. By 7:30, he said he was going to bed. Around 8:30, he got up and said he felt fine. He went out on the porch and ended up falling asleep there. I'm praying we hear from Hackensack tomorrow and that Bruce will feel well enough on Thanksgiving to enjoy the day.

Wednesday, 11/21:

Dr. G.'s nurse called this morning. She said Bruce is scheduled to begin the clinical trial on Tuesday. We have to be there by 7:00 a.m. so I made reservations at a nearby hotel for Monday night. Bruce will have blood work at 7:00 a.m.; an appointment with Dr. G at 8:00; trial infusion #1 after that; a four hour wait to be monitored; and then more blood work. He'll go back Wednesday and Thursday for blood work. That means I'll go for my Cat scans on Wednesday and then we'll head down to Hackensack. So next Tuesday, Wednesday, and Thursday are all medical days.

Thursday, 11/22:

Happy Thanksgiving! This was a rough day for Bruce. He didn't feel well throughout most of the day. Although he sat with us at dinner (And even ate more than usual.), the kids, the noise, and all the people got to him after a while. He went out on the sun porch to sit after dinner. On the positive side, Bruce and I DID spend another Thanksgiving together!

Tuesday, 11/27:

Bruce and I stayed at a hotel near the hospital last night. Thankfully, he felt fine this morning! We had breakfast and got to the Cancer Center by 7:00 a.m. We were there till 3:45. After blood work, we saw Dr. G. He said the last scan did show "some progression" of the disease. He said hopefully, the trial will keep it at bay. Bruce had several EKGs, blood pressures, temps, blood work, heart rates, etc., throughout the day. The infusion only lasted a half hour but everything else takes long and they have to adhere to a strict schedule, time-wise. Bruce and I are beyond grateful that he was able to begin the trial today. Now we'll pray that it helps to extend Bruce's life. Everyone at the Cancer Center was wonderful and Bruce handled everything like the champ he is!

Wednesday, 11/28:

I had my Cat scans this morning. Now I'll worry till the results are in. Bruce never worries. He said he's "too grateful for every day to worry about anything." He said he always expects good news from his scans. He also said that there's nothing to be afraid of since we know there's a Heaven and that life goes on. I don't know where this comes from with Bruce, but he always has total faith that everything will be fine. (For the record, I'm grateful for every day too. But I still worry.). From St. Clare's, we went to Hackensack for Bruce's blood work.

Thursday, 11/29:

Dr. Al called with very good news: my Cat scans are fine! I'm so relieved! Bruce went to Hackensack for his blood work this morning and was very happy to come home to good news for a change!

Friday, 11/30:

This morning I received a copy of my Cat scans. As Dr. Al told me, there's no new cancer. Thank God! However, it indicates "extensive scarring" on my right lower lung lobe and "some scarring" on the left lower lung lobe. With that, having lost two small parts of each lower lung lobe, and having pulmonary fibrosis, it's no wonder I cough all day long and experience occasional shortness of breath.

Tuesday, 12/4:

Bruce and I went to Hackensack for blood work and a doctor appointment. His blood work was fine. Regarding the pain Bruce nearly always has in his abdomen, the doctor suggested switching to Advil or Aleve rather than Tylenol.

Wednesday, 12/5:

Bruce vomited a lot this evening. He said everything he'd eaten all day came up. Of course, when something like this happens, I can't help but wonder if it's the cancer.

Friday, 12/7:

Bruce had terrible heartburn all night. He never had it this bad before. I gave him Pepto Bismal and he rested most of the day. I was worried this could be cancer related but he was fine by mid-morning.

Tuesday, 12/11:

Bruce and I arrived at the Cancer Center at 9:30 a.m. and didn't get out of there till 7:00 p.m. First he had blood work, which was fine. Then we had an appointment with Dr. G. If his pain worsens, they can either prescribe something stronger than Advil and/or recommend the pain management team they have there. After the doctor, we had to wait over a half hour for a chair to open up in the infusion room. Then we had to wait over an hour for the meds to be made and sent up from the pharmacy. The infusion itself is only a half hour but Bruce has to be monitored for four hours after it. It was a long, draining day. Thank Goodness we made the decision to stay overnight at the Hilton. Infusion #2 is now done; Bruce did fine with it!

Wednesday, 12/12:

Bruce went to bed before 8:00 tonight because his pain was so bad. I hate seeing this good man suffer so much.

Thursday, 12/13:

Bruce's pain was very bad today. He said on a scale of 1-10, it was a 7. But since he never complains, that 7 was probably a 10! Despite Bruce's pain, we still went to Colin's holiday concert. Bruce sat in the back and we left right after the first and second graders performed. Bruce mentioned that he knows the pain getting worse could be a sign of new tumors. As scary as this is for both of us, I had to admit that was true. After we got home from the concert, Bruce threw up and then began to feel much better.

Monday, 12/17:

Bruce and I met Pietrina and Anselmo at the Rockaway Diner for dinner this evening. Pietrina and Anselmo are two of our Wage Hope friends. Bruce felt fine and enjoyed the company and his meal. This was a lovely and welcomed evening after a very difficult week.

Tuesday, 12/18:

Bruce had blood work and a doctor appointment today. Dr. G prescribed pain meds for Bruce. He said we won't know what's causing Bruce's pain until his next Cat scan. I couldn't help wondering, however, if he does have an idea. Bruce picked up his barium for his Cat scan. Next week, he will go for infusion #3. The week after that, he doesn't have to go down to Hackensack at all.

Wednesday, 12/19:

Bruce had a very bad day and evening. He came home early from the gym because he was in too much pain to work out. This is the first time the pain hit him at the gym. Bruce said he was on the stairmaster when the pain kicked in. He got off of that and went on the treadmill. But he could only do it for five minutes. Besides the pain, Bruce said he just doesn't "feel right." He took meds and went to bed. He slept till around 10:00, got up, and then went to bed around 2:00 a.m. He couldn't eat and was nauseous. We had to skip Sean's Board of Education meeting this evening, where he was getting a certificate for making the high honor roll. It's so scary to see Bruce like this. I can't help but think the worst. A few months ago, he told me that the day he couldn't go to the gym would be the "beginning of the end" for him. I thought of that right away today. I told him to just try walking on the treadmill without elevating it. I think he'll try that tomorrow. God help us with this journey.

Thursday, 12/20:

Yesterday was a terrible day for Bruce but today was a very good day! He had very little pain and looked and felt much better than yesterday! He even went to the gym and walked on the treadmill for an hour. I'm hoping Bruce stays this way!

Friday, 12/21:

Bruce was in awful pain all day and throughout the evening. I felt so badly for him. I keep praying he'll feel better and have less pain.

Saturday, 12/22:

Bruce felt so much better today! He started taking CBD oil. I'm hoping that it helps him as much as it seems to help other people.

Sunday, 12/23:

Bruce and I met Doug for breakfast and then went to church with him. Today was another good day for Bruce—two days in a row! Thank you, God!

Monday, 12/24:

Carol, Doug, Bruce, and I went over to Chris and Jen's in the afternoon. We exchanged presents, had dinner, went to church (I wouldn't let Bruce go so he stayed at the house with Carol.), and then had dessert. Bruce did so well with everything! He looked good, he felt fine, he enjoyed the kids and the festivities, and he ate really well! This was a perfect Christmas Eve!

Tuesday, 12/25:

Merry Christmas!
Bruce's pain returned during the night and it was terrible! We were both up from around 1:00-3:00 a.m. Bruce went out on the porch and eventually, we both fell asleep. In the morning, he was still in pain. At one point, he said it was hard to breathe because he felt the pain by his lungs. That really scared me. He rested all morning and gradually began to feel better. Thankfully, he was well enough to drive to the cemetery so Carol and I could visit mom, dad, and other family members (Bruce stayed in

the car.). Then we went over to Debbie's for dinner. Bruce only ate a little and we left early but he made it for another lovely Christmas Day! For that, I'm beyond grateful!

Wednesday, 12/26:

Bruce and I went for his third infusion this morning. First he had blood work and then we had a doctor appointment. The doctor said that Bruce's pain could be the tumor hitting a nerve. Of course, we won't know for sure till the next Cat scan. When Bruce described the pain, the doctor said he should try OxyContin. Finally, Bruce agreed and the doctor gave us a prescription for it. He said to take Colace and Senocot for the constipation. Bruce's pain began to increase towards the end of his infusion—even while walking. By the time we got to the hotel, he was in terrible pain—the worst ever! It even hurt him to breathe. He lay on the floor for a little while. He felt like the pain was spreading. Some of it was brand new and came on suddenly. If Bruce can no longer go to the gym and/or go for his walks, he will slowly decline physically and emotionally. After two Tramadol and four Aleve, Bruce's pain finally eased up a little and he was able to sleep. For a while, I thought I was going to have to bring him back to the hospital. I'm just heartbroken over all of this!

Thursday, 12/27:

Somehow, Bruce and I both slept well last night. Bruce was very hungry so we had breakfast at the hotel. He began taking the OxyContin right after we got home. Thankfully, he didn't have any side effects and his pain lessened throughout the day. However, it seems to radiate when he lies down in certain positions. He said the pain pushes up towards his lungs. I'm so afraid this is a sign of new cancerous masses. We talked a little about death at dinner (Bruce only had a little soup.). Bruce said he wasn't "afraid of dying," but that he was "scared of not seeing Ella grow up." How sad but how sweet is that? That little girl surely has a hold on Bruce's heart.

Saturday, 12/29:

Bruce's pain was terrible this morning—he took a shower and doubled over. He felt like he was going to have a heart attack. I was so scared. I called Chris at 7:00 a.m., crying. I asked him if he'd drive us to the hospital if I drove to his house. He didn't hesitate. I woke Carol up to tell her what was going on. She called Michael, Doug, and Debbie. I called May on our way to the hospital. In the evening, I called Mark and Donna (From our NEGU group.) to tell them what was going on as they'd sent me a few messages.

After a long wait, Bruce was taken for a chest x-ray and Cat scans. The x-ray showed fluid in the right lung, which contributed to his pain. They drained most of it (Bruce told me later the pain was horrific.). The fluid was all red so it looked like there was blood all over the bed and Bruce's clothes. The Cat scan showed new, small tumors in Bruce's abdomen. Bruce had to be admitted to the hospital. Thank God Chris was with me. Around 4:00, Chris and I went back to his house and then I drove home. The thoracic doctor called and explained that when fluid from the lungs is red, it's a sign of cancer. Terrible news to hear. He said they will continue to drain the fluid.

Today was the scariest, saddest, and worst day yet in Bruce's fight with pancreatic cancer.

Sunday, 12/30:

Chris drove me to Debbie's this morning. Kelly picked me up and drove me to the hospital. Being a hospice nurse, she was such a big help— with Bruce and with me. Dr. Max, the doctor I spoke with last night, came in to go over everything. One of the oncologists we saw at the Cancer Center, also came in. She said that Bruce's thoracic issues have to be taken care of first. Then the oncology team will come in to discuss Bruce's cancer and where we go from here. Bruce is still in pain. It's heartbreaking.

Monday, 12/31:

Bruce called at 7:00 a.m. I could hardly understand him. He said he was having trouble breathing. Doug was in the kitchen with me when Bruce called. I had to wake Carol up and tell her we had to get to the hospital as soon as possible. Once again, I was beyond scared.

When we arrived at the hospital, Bruce was sitting in a chair and breathing better—what a huge relief! The doctor said he thought the breathing problems were "positional"—every time Bruce moves, it's harder to breathe. The doctor ordered head and chest Cat scans. The P/T came in and took Bruce for a little walk. He did very well. Carol and I went to the cafeteria for lunch while they took Bruce for his scans. Jen and Sean came in the afternoon and we were all there when Dr. Max came in to tell us about the Cat scans. The news is not good. Bruce has a blood clot on each lung. They've put him on Heparin. That only prevents new clots but doesn't dissolve clots. The body has to do that itself. If it doesn't, they have to go in surgically to do it. Dr. Max said they don't want it to come to that. They will test Bruce's legs to see if the clots came from there, which is common. The clots are cancer related. So much is happening at once. Dr. Max said the procedure to insert the chest tube is still scheduled for Wednesday morning. Bruce will be moved to the thoracic floor after that. Bruce's head scan was fine. Dr. Max was concerned about the breathing issues Bruce was having overnight and early this morning. He told Bruce he has to speak up when something's wrong. He told Bruce either he has a "high tolerance for pain" or is "too nice to complain." Jen and I said, "Both," at the same time. Dr. Max said that after he saw Bruce's x-ray, that showed the right lung filled with fluid, he didn't understand why Bruce wasn't "screaming with pain" at that point. I was glad he told Bruce that he has to speak up more. One thing Bruce did complain about was the bed. He can't sleep and had back and neck pain this morning because of it.

After I got home, around 8:00 p.m., Bruce called me and began to cry. Everything finally hit him and he said he's afraid to leave me, the family, and our friends. He said he doesn't want to miss seeing our grandchildren grow up. He even thanked me for all I've done for him. It absolutely broke my heart. I did my best to comfort him. A case worker came in at that time and Bruce gave the phone to her. She told me she would stay and talk with Bruce and that she'd also tell the nurse to give him a sedative this evening. I needed both a sleep aid and a tranquilizer to get to sleep.

PART FIVE

2019: January 1-17

Tuesday, 1/1:

A new year and probably a happy day for most people. For me, it was just another day of worrying about Bruce and what lies ahead. For Bruce, I'm sure today was much worse than it was for me.

Dr. Jeri called this morning to explain the procedure Bruce is having tomorrow. She agreed with Dr. Max that it's fine for me to stay home since Bruce will be out of the room for several hours. She'll call me as soon as the procedure is completed.

Doug brought me to the hospital and visited for quite a while. Dr. Paula came in while he was there. She said the oncology and research teams are all involved in Bruce's care. At this point, however, the thoracic issues have to be dealt with before the oncology issues are. She said these are all "hiccups" that can be handled one by one. I surely hope so.

Todd, from our Wage Hope group, visited today. Debbie and Michael came later on and stayed for a bit. Then they drove me to the Mall, where Chris picked me up and drove me home. This evening would be my first night home alone since Bruce's surgery three years ago.

Wednesday, 1/2:

Bruce called this morning. He sounded pretty good. It was a nerve wracking day for me, waiting for news about Bruce's surgical procedure.

Finally, around 1:00, Dr. Pete called. Sadly, the news is not good. They found more cancerous tumors in Bruce's chest. I was devastated. Also, they have to stop the Heperin because it was causing bleeding. They will now put filters in Bruce's legs to try to prevent more clots. The only good news is that they were able to "glue" something by Bruce's lungs to prevent fluid from backing up there. Dr. Pete said that Bruce's lungs expanded to normal size when he did this. Bruce's vitals are good and his heart is strong. There's a possibility he may have to go to rehab from the hospital. I'm fine with that and hopefully, Bruce will be as well.

A nurse called me this evening and said that Bruce asked him to call so he could talk to me. Bruce sounded really good! He said he could breathe deeply without pain and that they'd already gotten him up and walking. I felt so good hearing this! Later, after I'd just fallen asleep, Bruce called again. He still felt fine and just wanted to talk. This was the most he's talked to me since all of this started. I can't wait to see him tomorrow!

Thursday, 1/3:

Bruce called me three times today. Other than complaining about not being able to have any solid food, he sounded good.

Tonie and Jimmy drove me to the hospital. Tonie visited with Bruce for a little while. Doug left school early to come to the hospital. I was glad to have his company.

Several doctors came in while Doug and I were there. Bruce was nauseous and vomited while we were there so a Cat scan of the stomach may be ordered. Filters were inserted through Bruce's groin to prevent future clots from going to his heart. Dr. Jeri confirmed what Dr. Pete told me yesterday regarding the tumors in Bruce's chest. None of this is good.

Friday, 1/4:

Bruce called so Dr. G could talk to me. He said that all of the tubes have to be removed. Then an endoscopy may be ordered to see if there's a blockage in Bruce's bowel which would cause his nausea. After Bruce is released from the hospital, I have to make an appointment with Dr. G. He said we'll talk about what to do going forward. He said we definitely have to "change courses as the disease is progressing." I'm so very sad. Bruce got back on the phone. He realizes what's going on. I told him to just take things a day at a time and we'll handle whatever lies ahead. I'm not sure how, but we will.

JP drove me to the hospital today. Sandi was there when we got there. Lisa came later after the three of us had left. Bruce looked pretty good and was in good spirits. I had texted Dr. Al this morning to let him know Bruce has been in the hospital for a week and to ask him to call Dr. G for the details. Dr. Al called me while I was at the hospital. He said that Dr. G explained everything to him. I asked about chemo but he doesn't think it would help Bruce at this point. Dr. Al felt terrible about Bruce's setback.

A social worker said that Bruce will be evaluated before being released. He may be sent to a rehab or come home with home health care. There's a possibility he may need to be on oxygen. It looks like Bruce's lifestyle is going to change drastically after he comes home. I hope that doesn't depress him. Dr. Pete had told Bruce he'd be able to return to the gym in time but I seriously doubt that.

Saturday, 1/5:

Bruce was very agitated today. They didn't bring the air mattress to his new room (As I'd asked.) so he didn't sleep and his back and neck throbbed. To add insult to injury, the gastro doctors were in this morning to evaluate Bruce. They cleared him to be released. Bruce thought that meant he was coming home today. But the thoracic, pulmonary, and oncology doctors all have to evaluate him first before he can be released. Bruce has been in the hospital for eight days today and he's really ready to come home. Dr. Jeri removed the chest tube so Bruce is more comfortable now (Except for his back and neck.).

Mark and Donna, from our NEGU group, sent Bruce a beautiful blanket made up of numerous pictures of the family. It's such a thoughtful gift! I called Mark and Donna so Bruce and I could talk with them.

After I got home, Bruce called to tell me that Dr. Steve was in and said they want to keep Bruce there at least a couple more days. Dr. Steve told

Bruce he doesn't want anything to happen to him after he gets home and that then he has to return to the hospital.

Sunday, 1/6:

Henry and JP drove me to the hospital this morning. Bruce still has a lot of back and neck pain. I'd expected to go home with Henry and JP but things changed quickly. After Doug came, Bruce was cleared to go home. Unfortunately, he was not accepted to Home Health Care, which will make things very hard on me.The social worker told me that Bruce doesn't qualify because he doesn't need a walker, he's not on oxygen, and he doesn't have an open wound. So this is all going to be on my shoulders! After the paper work was completed, Bruce was ready to come home. Doug drove us, stopping at the drug store first in order to get Bruce's meds. By the time we got home, Chris was already here. He'd put the lights on for us. Then he helped Doug get Bruce into the house. After that, Chris took my car for gas. Doug stayed till we got settled and then went home. Chris and Doug have been great! I don't know what I'd do without them.

Monday, 1/7:

Bruce slept on the twin mattress topper on the porch floor last night. He just couldn't get comfortable on the twin bed, our bed, or the porch couch. Most of his pain is from his neck and lower back—he still thinks it's from the hospital bed. It's so sad to see him like this.

I made appointments with the thoracic surgeon, vascular surgeon, and Dr. G today. Dr. G.'s Physician Assistant called to check on Bruce.

I had to cancel Bruce's scheduled Cat scan for next week. I had already cancelled his dentist appointment for next week.

Tuesday, 1/8:

Bruce was still in pain today. He looks terrible and it's so sad. All he does is lie on the porch and watch t.v. He did eat a little today. He went downstairs to try the bed there. He liked it so he'll sleep there tonight. I'm so glad he won't have to sleep on the floor anymore. The only problem is that he has a lot of trouble breathing going up the stairs. I can't believe how quickly things have changed. My heart breaks for him.

Wednesday, 1/9:

Bruce slept downstairs last night but still was uncomfortable. Tonight he's going to sleep on the porch couch. He's in a lot of pain and is miserable. He's not eating much and it's beginning to show. His face looks so thin to me and sometimes his eyes look funny. He walks around the house with his cane every now and then but this is the exact opposite of what he's used to doing. He's always been so physically active. To watch him deteriorate like this is more heartbreaking than I can even put into words. As his caregiver, it's really hard on me to do everything. Debbie said this morning that she told Carol that she thinks sometimes people forget that I had two major surgeries this summer and that I'm dealing with my own health issues. This is difficult on so many levels. I just wish Bruce's pain would lessen.

Thursday, 1/10:

Bruce was in terrible pain all day and had difficulty breathing, even when he tried to walk. I put in a call to Dr. Al. I texted JP and he came over and checked Bruce's oxygen level, which was low. I called Dr. Al back and he told me to call 911, which I did. I also called Dr. G. The police came and put Bruce on an oxygen mask. Then the paramedics arrived. They took Bruce to St. Clare's by ambulance. JP drove me to the hospital (God bless him!). Dr. Al called ahead to tell the hospital that Bruce was coming. Before JP and I left, I had called Jen to fill her in and to ask her to let the family know what was going on. Doug left school as soon as he got Jen's text and came straight to the hospital. JP left a little while after Doug got there. Doug spent the next seven hours in the Emergency Room with me. They did a Cat scan on Bruce and found more fluid build-up in the right lung. That means the procedure where they put some kind of "glue" by the lung to prevent fluid build-up didn't work. Now Bruce has to have another chest tube inserted,which he's dreading. Once Bruce was finally admitted and in a room, Doug and I left. It was after 9:00 p.m. at that point. While we were in the E.R., Bruce told Doug and me that he doesn't know "how much more" he can take. While that's totally understandable, it's also very scary to me. For the first time in three years, Bruce seems to be giving up. Doug and I did our best to find the right words to say to him. Neither of us gave him any of the usual positive platitudes. I want Bruce here for a long time. But I definitely understand his discouragement and depression.

Friday, 1/11:

Bruce's Whipple was three years ago today. Now he's back at the hospital where it all started. I'm heartbroken.

Bruce called me at 5:15 a.m. I really got scared. He was very down. I told him not to give up; to just take things a day at a time until we know what's going on.

JP picked me up this morning and drove me to the hospital. While he was there, Franco came to talk to Bruce. JP and I waited in the hall to give them privacy. Franco is a great guy besides being a pancreatic cancer survivor and a pastor. I was so grateful he took the time to visit and talk with Bruce. He told me that he told Bruce that he's been the strong one for all of us but that now he has to let everyone be strong for him. I'm so grateful Franco visited today and talked with Bruce for over a half hour.

Bruce looks terrible, is in a lot of pain, is very nauseous, isn't eating much, is very quiet, and still seems very depressed to me. It's the exact opposite of how he normally is and so very sad to witness. He also threw up while JP and I were there. The pulmonologist came in and said Bruce doesn't have much fluid in his lung and definitely not enough to drain. He doesn't know what's causing Bruce's pain. Bruce's white blood count is low, indicating an infection. They don't know what that is yet. We'll have to wait for the blood test results. They put Bruce on an antibiotic. He's also back on oxygen.

The case manager came in to talk to us. She said that Bruce qualifies for home health care and that she'll set it up when he's released. Later, someone from the Visiting Nurse Association came in to explain their services. Bruce will need oxygen at home.

Bruce had a lot of visitors today, though he didn't interact with any of them. May's been keeping Bill posted and he decided to drive up with his son so he can see Bruce. They live in Florida and are going to drive straight through. They left today. I thought that would cheer Bruce up but he didn't even react when I told him Bill was coming up. May asked Bruce if it was okay for Bill to visit and Bruce just nodded yes. Michael called and offered to come home for a weekend.

Saturday, 1/12:

I called Bruce this morning and he sounded just like himself from the moment he said, "Hello." What a difference a day makes! He said that the pain meds are being given more frequently and that has made all the difference. He felt good and was talking like nothing was wrong. I was thrilled! He wants Dr. Al back in charge of his care. Good for Bruce for making decisions about his own health care!

Dr. Russ, the pulmonologist, and Dr. Tom, an oncologist, came in while Doug and I were with Bruce. Dr. Russ said that Bruce's lungs sound clear. Dr. Tom didn't have such good news—Bruce's tumor markers (CA-19) are over 5,000–the highest they've been. Clearly, the cancer has spread.

Gordon, who's a P/T and from our Wage Hope group, took the train to the hospital. He stayed a long time and gave us lots of good advice for when Bruce comes home. Lisa, another one of our Wage Hope friends and a pancreatic cancer survivor, came to visit right after Gordon left. After I'd gotten home,Bruce called and said: "That Lisa's a piece of work!" Then he laughed, which was so good for me to hear!

The physical therapist came to evaluate Bruce, to walk with him with a walker, and to have him do a stepper. The P/T said that Bruce's oxygen dropped after walking a short distance but that it quickly went up to 90 after he sat down. He agrees that Bruce needs oxygen at home. He's going to put in an order for a walker. Bruce will have p/t at home. Doug bought me a pulse odometer so I'll be able to check Bruce's oxygen levels in between visits from the home health aide.

Jen visited Bruce today. Shortly after she arrived, Wayne, May, Bill, and Bill's son, Chris, all came. Bill and Chris drove up from Florida to see Bruce. Then Pietrina and her husband, Anselmo, came. So we had a roomful of visitors. The nurses asked if we were having a party! We wouldn't have been able to have everyone in the room if Bruce had had a roommate. Doug made a beautiful and very special video of all of us with Bruce (See waginghopewithbruce.com).

Sunday, 1/13:

When Doug and I got to the hospital this morning, Bruce was in a lot of pain, couldn't get comfortable, was very irritable, and was very depressed. What a difference a day makes! Bruce said he hopes the family won't be "disappointed" in him since he's decided not to pursue any more clinical trials and won't do chemo unless there's something that can really help him. I assured him no one could ever be disappointed in him. He's been the strongest person we know, especially throughout the past three years.

A respiratory therapist came in while Doug and I were there. She said it's obvious that Bruce needs oxygen. He's on it there and will need it at home.

Chris and the boys visited after Doug left. At one point, while they were there, Bruce told me I'd "better call Leber" (Leber-Lakeside Funeral Home, our local funeral home). Then he asked me if I was "going to be okay." Heartbreaking.

Wayne, May, and Laurie visited today. Wayne and May couldn't believe the difference in Bruce between yesterday and today. I'm glad Bruce's one good day was when his family was there.

I've been getting several phone calls, texts, and facebook messages. Everyone is heartbroken over Bruce's setback.

After I got home, I called the nurse's station at 7:15 p.m. because the nurse I like leaves at 7:30. She said that Bruce fell asleep after we all left and that he slept for over an hour. She said that he told her his pain is still there but isn't as bad as it's been all day.

Monday, 1/14:

A thoracic surgeon came in today and said there's enough fluid in Bruce's right lung to be drained. That's different from what the pulmonologist said. This doctor said that Bruce needs a catheter, which will be permanent. The case manager came in to talk about what we need for Bruce when he comes home. The physical therapist came to walk with Bruce. She said he can only do 40 feet without getting out of breath. He's gone from one extreme to the other and it's beyond sad.

Chris and Doug both visited Bruce today. They agreed with me that Bruce was much more alert today.

Tuesday, 1/15:

Henry drove me to the hospital this morning and stayed for a couple of hours. Thankfully, he stayed till Dr. Al got there as the news isn't good. The cancer has spread to Bruce's lungs and stomach. There's nothing that can be done. Dr. Al recommended Hospice and we agreed to it. They may come to the house tomorrow to set up. Henry kept me calm throughout Dr. Al's very emotional talk. The hospice ladies and case manager all came to talk to me. I can't believe we've reached this point. I'm just numb.

Bruce was moved to the oncology ward on the third floor. He's in so much pain and is very agitated. He understands that the end is near.

Doug and his friend, Marc, went to the hospital this evening after I had left. Doug told me later that when Marc left, he told Bruce he didn't know when he'd see him again. Bruce said: "I'll see you in Heaven." That was like someone just punched me in my heart.

Bruce's cousin, Jeff, called to ask about Bruce. His family is dealing with their daughter-in-law's breast cancer. She's only 33 and has three children under seven, including a one year old. I hate this disease so much! It hurts so many good people and destroys so many loving families.

Wednesday, 1/16:

There's so much going on, my head is spinning. A nurse called about bringing Bruce home. He was supposed to come home today but I'd have to get to Rockaway to get his morpheme and I couldn't arrange that. So he'll come home tomorrow instead. The social worker called. I couldn't go to the hospital because I had to wait for the hospice team to come and make the arrangements for Bruce to come home. The hospice bed and equipment arrived in the afternoon and was set up. I have it all on the sun porch, Bruce's favorite room.

I called the hospital while Doug was there and Bruce actually got on the phone. He said hello to me in a strong voice. He did say he hadn't had a good day. Of course, that made me sad. I wish I could've been with Bruce today.

Jake sent me a few very cute texts. I know he's aware of what's going on. He even asked me if I was "alright." So sweet.

I texted Dr. Al and asked him to call me, which he later did. He thinks the cancer spread while Bruce was on the immune therapy but he said there's no way that would've caused it. He doesn't think Bruce has long to live. My heart is breaking. Later, Dr. Al texted about our blog. He went on it and said that Bruce will be leaving an "amazing legacy." I certainly agree.

Thursday, 1/17:

Dr. Al's nurse called. She thinks Bruce should be in Dover's Hospice rather than at home. She wanted me to get to the hospital to discuss it. I called Chris and he picked me up and drove me over there. Bruce looked terrible—so much worse than on Tuesday, when I last saw him. I don't think he's going to last much longer. He's spitting up bile, his cheeks are sunken in, and he's "in and out." He did ask me if I was "going to be okay." It was hard not to cry. Bruce seemed to understand about being moved to hospice and seemed to be okay with it. An associate of Dr. Al's came in and said Bruce has to go to hospice. I was concerned about making the wrong decision—whether to bring him home as planned or put him in hospice. The decision was made for me, which was helpful. The Compassionate

Care social worker, T.J., looked at Bruce and then spoke to Chris and me privately. He explained everything. We went back to be with Bruce while TJ made the necessary arrangements for hospice. After that, TJ told us to go home and that he'd call when Bruce was settled in at the hospice.

After we got home, JP came over so I told him the latest. Everyone was expecting Bruce to come home today.

I called Leber-Lakeside Funeral Home and talked with Joe, who knows Bruce well as Bruce used to dog sit for him. I wanted him to know that Bruce is terminal. Joe knew about Bruce's cancer and was sorry to hear how it had progressed. He said what a great guy Bruce is and how much he always liked him. He told me Bruce had told him many times that he wanted to be cremated and that he didn't want a Wake. So Joe already knew what I was asking of him. I'm just so sorry it's come to this.

Kelly called. She was at the hospital and told me when Bruce was being transported to the hospice. TJ called when they got there. I found out later that Bruce thanked the nurses for taking care of him. That's so like him. Even at the end, he was thinking of others. Kelly told me that Bruce also said to the nurses: "It's time for me to go."

Chris put up a beautiful post about Bruce being moved to hospice, along with a very touching video of Ella, on FaceBook. I got numerous responses from it.

After TJ called to tell me Bruce was at their hospice and settled in, Henry and JP picked me up and we went over there. Bruce wasn't responsive and he looked terrible. He opened his eyes once and asked where he was so I told him. The nurse told me that he only said one thing to her—that he's a Mets' fan. Bruce did like the Mets but he was definitely more of a Yankee fan! Doug came to the hospice right from school. He took off tomorrow so he can be with Bruce and me. Henry and JP went home after Doug got there. JP told Doug to call him during the night if we needed him. Kelly and one of the nurses both said they thought Bruce would make it through the night. Debbie, Michael, and Gianna came to visit Bruce. It was so very sad. The night nurse, Cory, told me to go home and get some rest. He said he'd call if there was even a change in Bruce. So Doug and I reluctantly left. Doug took my cell phone in the bedroom with him so that I could sleep. That didn't happen.

Around 11:40 p.m., Cory called my cell but Doug didn't pick up in time. Cory left a message to call him but when Doug called back, the phone kept ringing. Then Cory called my house phone and I picked up immediately. I got the news I'd been dreading. Bruce passed away at 11:30 p.m., peacefully, Thursday, 1/17/19. I was a mess and so was Doug. So Doug called JP and he came to pick us up (And it was snowing.). I called Chris in the car and got his machine. He met us at the hospice. Doug called Debbie. She and Mike attempted to drive to the hospice but route 80 was too bad because the plows hadn't been out yet. They had no choice but to turn around. I called May on our way to the hospice. She offered to come down but I told her not to because of the weather.

Douglas and I went into Bruce's room together. JP waited in the hall to give us some privacy. It was terrible to see Bruce like that. He was still warm. I touched his arm and kissed his forehead. His mouth was open. Otherwise, he just looked like he was sleeping. Doug was very emotional but he still managed to calm me down and to say all of the right things. I was feeling so guilty that I had left the hospice and wasn't there when Bruce passed. Chris and JP came into the room. Both of them were very emotional. Bruce was so loved! Chris called Michael and he picked up right away. Afterwards, I got a beautiful text from Michael. At the end of the text, Michael said he hoped he could be "half the father" to his kids that Bruce was to him, Chris, and Doug. What a beautiful tribute from a stepson to a stepfather! We were there till around 2:00 a.m. When we left, one of the nurses told me she knew Bruce because he was her pet-sitter. I was glad that Bruce had a familiar face with him at the end.

The snow had let up by the time we left and the plows had been out so we didn't have any trouble getting home. I'm just numb. Even with all of the treatment, Bruce barely lasted three years. Everything came to an end at the beginning of December. From then on, things kept getting progressively worse. Bruce always said this disease wasn't going to kill him. Sadly, tonight, the disease won. I can't imagine what life will be like without him.

Bruce, you were the most spiritual, the bravest, most positive, loyal, genuine, and loving person I've ever known. You were also the kindest and most compassionate person I've ever known. You loved me unconditionally and without reservation for thirty years. You were an amazing step-father to Michael, Chris, and Doug! You did so much for those boys and never expected anything in return. My mother used to say that when you died you were going to "Step-father Heaven"! If there is such a place, you certainly earned it! And if there's a special Heaven for spouses, you deserve that too. You brought me renewed life and joy all those years ago. You stayed by my side throughout four difficult surgeries of my own and throughout my own cancer battle. You worried more about me than yourself. Actually, you worried more about everyone than yourself. There wasn't anything you wouldn't do to help a fellow human being, whether you knew them or not. You cared for and loved every animal that crossed your path, especially dogs. And they always returned your love! More than anything else, you taught all of us not only how to live but how to die. You were truly a Gift—my Gift! Thank you for loving me and for thirty wonderful years!

Rest In Peace, Bruce.

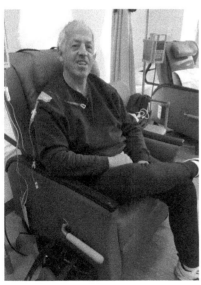

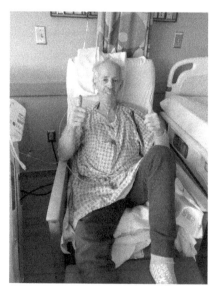

PART SIX

Supplements to Bruce A. Hill: Pancreatic Cancer Warrior

BRUCE A. HILL: OBITUARY

On Thursday, January 17th, 2019, Bruce Allen Hill passed away at the age of 65 after a heroic three-year battle with pancreatic cancer. Bruce was born on May 15th, 1953, in Somerville, New Jersey, to Vincent Hill and Hilda Sargent Hill. Highly regarded for his strong work ethic, impeccable character, and giving spirit, Bruce often credited his upbringing in the small town of Peapack-Gladstone, New Jersey as the source of his deeply entrenched value system. After a standout baseball career as a pitcher at Watchung Hills Regional High School, Bruce was drafted by the Kansas City Royals where he played in their farm system.

At the end of his athletic career, Bruce worked as a landscaper, running his own business, Green Hills Lawn Service. After marrying Linda, his beloved wife of 30 years. Bruce moved to his second home, Hopatcong, New Jersey, where he launched his career as a professional pet sitter. Running his own pet sitting business for two decades, Bruce quickly became a celebrity in and around Hopatcong and was highly regarded for his professionalism, compassion, and strong gift for working with pets of any variety, but especially dogs.

After retiring, Bruce worked equally hard as a tireless volunteer and advocate for the Pancreatic Cancer Action Network. Through his efforts with PANCAN, Bruce was able to touch lives across the country, and even internationally, as he inspired countless people to fight their sickness with the same combination of faith, hope, and positivity that Bruce used to fight his own.

Bruce was preceded in death by his father, Vincent, his mother, Hilda, brother Bob, sisters-in-law Ann and Sue, close friend, Roger Haskell, and dear family friend, Maureen Schmidt. Bruce will also be lovingly welcomed by his countless canine friends, but especially Max, Necco, Scout, Zoe, Puffy, Jacques, and Jeter. Bruce is survived by his wife, Linda, her three sons, Michael, Christoper, and Douglas, daughters-in-law Jen and Laura, grandchildren Sean, Jake, Colin, Ella, Judson, Dominic, and Anna, brothers Bill, Wayne, and Ron, sisters-in-law May and Marge, and several nieces and nephews. In addition, his loving care will be missed by the many dogs who survived him, especially Piper, Luca, and Buddy.

Donations can be made to the Pancreatic Cancer Action Network in Bruce's name.

Eulogy: Written by Douglas Palermo

Good morning. Thank you for coming out for Bruce today. That alone would be enough of a tribute to the life of Bruce Hill, but I've had the pleasure of being at my mom's side as her phone exploded with text message after text message, Facebook alert after Facebook alert, as she read all of the beautiful testimonies of what Bruce meant to so many people. The outpouring of love and support showered on my family these past few very difficult days has been humbling, and I wanted to thank everybody for that. As I sat down to write this I couldn't think of what more I could possibly say about Bruce Hill that hasn't already been said. But I'll try.

It's very difficult trying to make sense of how somebody so good would be taken from us so soon, when he had so much more to experience, and give, and teach us. What I have been trying to tell myself to make sense of it is that Bruce didn't die young, he graduated early. As a lifelong teacher coming from a family of teachers, I tend to see the whole world as just one big classroom. And if that is the case, then I can think of no better student of life than Bruce Hill.

Very early in his life Bruce was taught some very important lessons. If you would have asked him, he would have credited growing up in the small town of Peapack-Gladstone for teaching him everything he needed to know, but I'm sure specifically it was his mom and his brothers that had the most influence over him. Either way, at some point early in his life, Bruce was taught three important lessons: Be a good person, work hard, and help others. And Bruce learned those lessons quickly and never swayed from them an inch his entire life. Be good. Work hard. Help others. He didn't need to study at any prestigious university, read any self-help books, or sit at the feet of any gurus to figure out how to live his life. He already knew. Be good. Work hard. Help others.

But school unfortunately is not just about learning lessons; it's also about being tested to ensure that you know what you're supposed to know. And Bruce was truly tested by this world.

When his father died when Bruce was only three and he had to grow up never knowing or having any memories of his dad, he easily could have grown bitter and angry at the world. But he didn't. He just remembered his lessons. Be good. Work hard. Help others.

When he was one step away from living his dream of pitching in the Major Leagues and his arm goes dead, he easily could have turned cold. Bars are populated with failed athletes living in the past unable to deal with broken dreams. But not Bruce. He just returned home and remembered his lessons. Be good. Work hard. Help others.

When he finally found the love of his life and his mom died mere months before she could dance with her youngest son at his wedding, Bruce just soldiered on and took all the love his mom gave him and showered it on his wife for the next thirty years. Be good. Work hard. Help others.

When his first dog, Max, whom he loved and cared for with every particle of his being, turned on him, biting the hand that fed him, and had to be put down too soon, Bruce could have soured on the idea of having another dog. But he didn't just double down, he tripled down with three more dogs: Scout, Necco, and Zoe that brought so much joy in his life for years.

And when his body could no longer handle the daily toil of doing the job he loved for so long, being a landscaper, he effortlessly pivoted into being a pet sitter, the career where Bruce could finally show that he wasn't just a strong person on the outside, he was a deeply loving, caring, empathetic person on the inside. Be good. Work hard. Help others.

When his wife was diagnosed with renal cancer, he stood by her side like a rock as she dealt with having a kidney removed and went through the physically and emotionally taxing recovery that followed.

And when he received the most devastating diagnosis one can receive from a doctor: pancreatic cancer, he didn't feel sorry for himself for a moment. He just immediately began preparing for what he knew would be the fight of his life. Be good. Work hard. Help others.

When he pretty much had his entire insides removed in a 10-hour Whipple Surgery, it was less than four months later that he completed a 5K through the steep hills of Hopatcong—not for himself or his disease—but for his hero, Dylan Flinchum, a young boy who Bruce continually credited for the source of his own massive strength and determination.

And when Maureen Schmidt, a truly dear friend to Bruce, my mom, and the whole family, tragically passed away the very same day Bruce was told that his cancer had returned, we all were ready to throw up our hands, wave the white flag, and give up to this cruel world. But not Bruce. He just turned his grief into the strength and courage necessary for the next stage of his battle. And we all had no choice but follow his lead. Be good. Work hard. Help others.

Just this past year, when his wife's cancer returned and she had to face two major surgeries; when his daughter-in-law got diagnosed with breast cancer and had to face her own fight; when his own cancer was no longer responding to chemo and was beginning to grow and spread, Bruce remained strong. Bruce remained positive. Bruce remained an inspiration to all of us.

And these last couple of weeks, when we had to witness Bruce endure more pain and discomfort than anybody should ever have to, yet we never saw him get anymore agitated or grumpy than the average person before they had their first cup of coffee. Right up to the end. When all of his thoughts were on the people he was leaving behind and not a single one for himself. He didn't wait until he was ready to leave, he waited for ALL OF US to be ready before he left. Be good. Work hard. Help others.

Bruce was once told that him having cancer was like taking one for the team—and he was always reassured by that idea. Bruce rarely talked openly about his faith, but he was a deeply spiritual person. His faith was just as simple, yet just as firm and deep-rooted as all the other pillars he stood on. He simply loved God and followed the Platinum Rule of loving others like God loves us all. And loving others like God loves us requires sacrifice, it requires us all to be willing to carry our own crosses. And that's what Bruce did with his disease. He willingly took upon the cross of pancreatic cancer so that we all could learn from him, be inspired by him, and become better people because of him. And we did. We did learn from him. We were inspired by him. We are better people because of him.

So I say, Thank You, Bruce. Thank you for all you did and all you sacrificed for all of us. We are all forever in your debt. I promise that I will not allow your death to be a tragedy. I will continue to carry on your legacy by embodying the lessons you learned so young and lived so effortlessly. I will be good. I will work hard. I will help others. And I know I'm not alone.

Thank you.

Speeches Given at Bruce Hill's Celebration of Life: March 2, 2019

Linda Hill:

When Bruce first told me he didn't want a traditional Wake, I suggested a Celebration of Life instead. He asked me what that was so I explained what I knew about it. He listened and looked at me and said: "Do you think anyone would come?" I said: "Are you kidding? For you, everyone will come." Thank you all for proving me right and being here today.

There are several people I need to thank.

First of all, none of this would be possible without Henry's help, so thank you, Henry. I'd like to thank everyone who donated food, made our centerpieces, or helped with setting up. Many of you have been here since early this morning. There are too many to name but I appreciate all of you. Doug not only wrote Bruce's obituary and eulogy, and designed our program and bracelets, and did our slide show, but he and his friend, Marc, made a beautiful video which you'll see shortly. Jen did our picture boards and the framed picture of Bruce. Chris and Jen bought all of the items for the kids. Chris will be our DJ today. Bob assisted with our audio. I'd like to thank our Purple Family, whom Bruce loved so much, for their support of Bruce and me, for their visits to the hospital, and for their unending advocacy for pancreatic cancer. Equally involved in advocating for pancreatic cancer is my Never Ever Give Up group, some of whom drove eight hours to be here today.

Bruce's brother, Wayne, and his wife, May, were at the hospital with Bruce every day just as they were when he had his surgery. Another brother drove with his son straight through from Florida to see Bruce. The day they got to the hospital was Bruce's last good day.

Debbie, Michael, and Gianna were with us at the Hospice on Bruce's last day. They tried to come back after Doug called to tell them about Bruce but it was snowing and they were forced to turn around. My sister stayed with me for two weeks after Bruce passed, stocking up my freezer so she knew I'd have something to eat after she left.

As most people know, Dylan Flinchum was Bruce's super hero. He gave Bruce strength to fight these past three years. Any time Bruce had a setback, he'd always say the same thing: "This is nothing compared to what Dylan goes through." Dylan was supposed to be here today but he had a setback of his own recently and could use our prayers. Dylan's four grandparents are here. By the way, I'm sure if Bruce were here he'd tell all of you that you should attend Dylan's next Dinosaur Stomp on May eleventh.

More than anyone, I have to thank my family here by my side, as they've been for Bruce and me throughout the past four difficult years. A special thank you to Doug, Chris, and my fourth son, J.P. I would not have made it through the terrible night of January 17th and the early morning hours of the 18th without them. They were beyond amazing!

In the past four years, I was diagnosed with cancer and underwent three major surgeries. Bruce was diagnosed with cancer and underwent surgery, numerous rounds of chemo and radiation, and a brief try with a clinical trial. Laura had chemo, radiation, and surgery after her own cancer diagnosis, and she'll have another surgery this summer. Chris underwent an emergency appendectomy. Jake was hospitalized with a serious illness that lasted months and left him unable to walk for a while. Ella was hospitalized as an infant with a serious virus. And not to be outdone, Colin had to be rushed to the hospital after a terrible accident outside his school. All the while, the constant in my life and the person who kept me sane was Bruce. He would always say, "This is just a bump in the road." Then he'd assure me that everything would be alright. I have Cat scans every three months and the week after next, I face my first scan without Bruce by my side to reassure me. Fortunately, Chris is going to take me for my scans. I'm hoping Bruce's strength and positivity will get me through whatever lies ahead.

Finally, as much as I appreciate all of you being here, and I do, if you really want to honor Bruce, live your life as he did—be kind and care about others.

Thank you.

Michael Palermo:

Ever since my stepfather, Bruce, passed away, I've thought about what I might want to say to honor him at his life celebration. I could talk about his courageous battle with cancer, his devotion to my mother, the joy he found in being a grandparent, or the many ways he enriched our community. I decided, though, that I would share something more personal about what Bruce meant to me. The circumstances in which Bruce came into my life were not exactly auspicious. I was thirteen years old at the time. I was angry and sad and in no mood to welcome Bruce into our home. In my best moments, I was indifferent to what in retrospect was his incredible kindness, patience, and generosity towards me. At my worst, I took my anger out on him. He never complained, he never responded in kind, and continued to go above and beyond what would have been expected of anyone else in a similar position. I hope he knows how much I appreciated him, even though I would have never dared say it out loud at the time. I think he does because I know of no one who was filled with more pure, genuine good than Bruce. I will miss him, of course, but he will be with me as I continue to strive to be the kind of father, husband, and selfless human being he always was.

Christopher Palermo:

I was eleven years old in the Spring of 1987 the first time I met Bruce. That's a year younger than my oldest son, Sean, is now. And Bruce—he was a fresh-faced 33–a decade younger than I am now. My life was pretty simple back then. I was finishing up fifth grade—spent most of my money on baseball cards; spent most of my time playing wiffleball. I was an avid baseball fan growing up. The type of kid who ran out first thing in the morning hoping the newspaper was delivered so I could check the box scores to see how my favorite teams and players fared the night before. I'm not sure if anyone even does that anymore. I'm not sure they even deliver newspapers anymore…

But it was my love of baseball that contributed to my first impression of Bruce. As most of you know, Bruce was a standout pitcher at Watchung Hills. One of my favorite stories—if you can call it that—was about the times they played Summit High School and Bruce had to pitch against Willie Wilson, who was a couple grades below him. Willie was a man-child who would go on to become a 2-time major league All-Star and World Series champion with the Kansas City Royals. I remember one time in the car with Bruce—it was just the two of us—and I asked him about facing Willie and how he fared against him. Bruce didn't even turn to me, he just shook his head, laughed to himself, and said, "Ohhh boy…oooooo." And that was it! I was waiting on the edge of my seat to get the play by play, the breakdown of pitches, what it was like staring him down, but that was all I got. That was Bruce. To this day, I don't know if Willie lit him up or if Bruce found a way to strike him out. I always like to think it was the latter—And that's the version I've told people during my retelling of the story. Like the saying goes, "When the legend becomes fact, print the legend."

But that legend was nothing Bruce pushed. Despite being signed by the Royals out of high school (possibly by the same scouts who were sent to see Will) and playing professional baseball, you would never know it. There's an important life lesson there—the humility and selflessness that Bruce had. He loved sports and talked sports a lot—but all of his personal stories were about the athletic achievements and accomplishments of the rest of the Hill family. Rarely about himself. Now I don't know about you, but if I was signed to play pro ball out of high school, that would be my opening line for the rest of my life! But he never made it about himself. He was always about everyone else. During his ER visit to Hackensack in January, I drove Bruce that day—he was in a lot of pain. And the first thing he said when I got into the car? Bruce apologized for pulling me away from whatever I had going on that day. I told Bruce that he's been there so many times that I needed him over the years and not once did he ever say no, or that he was too busy—so it was time for me to be there for him now. When the doctor came into the ER room, he looked at my mom and asked Bruce who she was. Bruce said, "That's my wife." Then the doctor pointed to me and asked who I was. Bruce looked at me and said, "He's my Chris." That meant so much to me.

Now back to 1987. It was one of the first times he came over our house. My brothers and I were outside in our yard with some neighborhood friends playing wiffleball. That was pretty much the neighborhood game for us until snow football season came around. As we're playing, Bruce walked out of the house to watch us play. One of my friends stole a glance at Bruce, then turned to me with a shocked look on his face, whispering, "Do you see the size of his forearms??!" Like I said, Bruce was only 33, not far off the prime of his physicality. His forearms were more jacked than most people's legs. Though he spent time in the gym, Bruce had what some would call "farmer strength." The type of muscle and strength you can never get inside a gym or with expensive supplements. The type you can only get from living a very physical life, which he did. And that physicality and strength never left him. Back when Bruce had his Whipple surgery where they removed part of his pancreas, part of his small intestine, his appendix, his gall bladder, and his spleen—five major organs in a ten hour surgery! Doug and I were worrying how the heck we'd get Bruce up two flights of stairs at home after he was discharged. What does Bruce do when we get home? He walks up both flights completely on his own strength. It was incredible—and just the first of many examples of both outer and inner strength Bruce showed during his fight—and that strength never left him.

I'm sure many of you have shaken Bruce's hand at some point over the years. If you haven't, when he shook your hand, it felt like you were shaking the hand of an NFL lineman. His bear paws swallowed me up—not just when I was a kid but even during his final days. I remember thinking the last time in the hospital when I shook his hand to say goodbye that whatever cancer took from Bruce's insides, it couldn't touch that mighty grip of his on the outside.

But back to sports—Our mutual love of sports was always a big part of our relationship. Bruce took me to my first NFL game, my first NHL game, and of course, there were lots of baseball games together. Most notably, the first time I went to Yankee stadium with Bruce—we went to see the Yankees and the Blue Jays. After we got inside the stadium, Bruce led us towards the Blue Jays' bullpen. When we got there, he shouted down to the pitching coach. The coach, who apparently Bruce knew, stopped what he was doing, looked up into the stands where we were, and greeted Bruce with a big, welcoming smile as they proceeded to have a conversation. When you're a kid and you're with someone who is talking to the players or coaches on the field of a Major League Baseball game—that leaves a pretty big impression.

In addition to the games that Bruce took me to as a kid, I had had the opportunity to take him to one much later in life. This past summer, the boys and I took Bruce out to a Red Bulls' soccer match at Red Bull Arena in Harrison. He mentioned to us earlier that year that he'd wanted to see the arena and watch a match. So we made sure it happened that summer—me, Bruce, Doug, and the boys. He loved it—though being a former professional landscaper and someone who was beyond meticulous with his own lawn till the very end—I think he was more impressed with the quality and maintenance of the grass than he was with the actual match. As we were walking out, I told Bruce, "Well you can cross that one off of your bucket list." That was one of the last few items he did cross off that list but what was so incredible about Bruce—from the time he was diagnosed, it wasn't just the soccer match, he must've done about ten 5Ks, trips to D.C., one-in-a-lifetime concerts to see Streisand and Paul McCartney, the blog and his videos with Doug, his continual visits to the gym—he NEVER let cancer stop him. He never let cancer slow him down.

Among all of those sports-related memories, the one I'll hold closest to my heart was the two years that Bruce and I had season tickets for Rutgers Football. Going to games during that two year stretch was one of the few times in my life when it was just me and Bruce. We shared the car ride down for an hour. The four hours at the game. The hour back. One of the main reasons we got season tickets was to watch Hopatcong's own, Joe Martinek, during his Junior and Senior years. Often, Bruce and I would tailgate with the Martineks and the families of the other players. It was like a sports fantasy camp that we got to experience together week after week for two years in the Fall. Bruce and I would always wear our matching #38 MARTINEK jerseys—which I custom made. We became very close to the Martineks and I know Bruce loved watching Joe play, not just because he was from our Town and we knew the family but because Bruce loved the work ethic Joe had. A very similar non-stop fighting attitude when people said you can't do it, he'd say watch me. Bruce showed that some fighting attitude after he got sick.

The day I posted on Facebook about Bruce passing away, I got many messages. One in particular hit me because it reminded me of that time that Bruce and I shared together. It was from Joe Martinek's Dad. The text read:

"I'm at the gym reading your post about Bruce; couldn't even see the words anymore because of the tears. My heartfelt condolences to you, your mom, and the entire family. When someone wears your son's name on his back, not because he's great, but because he's proud to know him, your heart breaks when a man like Bruce passes. Goddamn tears won't stop. This workout is for him! You're in my thoughts and prayers…"

A few days before Bruce left us, I took all three boys to visit him at the hospital. I knew we were nearing the end so it was important for me to make sure I brought them. It would end up being their final time seeing Bruce. He was fading in and out that day. But the times he was awake and alert, I could tell he was happy to see the boys. And he asked many questions about Sean's tennis tournament the day before and Jake's and Colin's winter soccer. Genuinely interested. Even at the end, it was never about him; it was about everyone else. I am convinced that Bruce had three strong years living with Pancreatic Cancer not because he was fighting for himself but because he wanted to fight for everyone else. He knew how much his story meant to all of us.

I'll miss seeing him on the sidelines of the boys' sporting events because he was a constant fixture—home, away, didn't matter. He was always there. Even after he got sick—most people after chemo, they'd go home and go to bed to rest. Not Bruce. He was back out there on the fields to give his support. And I have a feeling he'll still be watching over them and cheering them on—whether it be Sean's tennis matches, Jake or Colin's soccer matches, and Ella—well I'm not sure what she'll be doing but even if it's six-hour dance recitals, I'm sure Bruce will be there watching over every minute of his girl.

I'd like to close with a post that I put up on Facebook a couple years back. Throughout Bruce's fight I posted many times about what was going on, how it was affecting my kids and the family. But this one from

2017 still seems to resonate because it epitomized the way Bruce lived his life—making the most until the very end. It read…

"The other day we had the Palermo quartet serenade Papa Bruce with their rendition of Happy Birthday in honor of Bruce's big day on Monday. Feels like life has flashed by so quickly these last few years. I can't even tell you the point at which I hit that transition from growing up to growing old. But that's something I think about with each birthday that rolls around. That it means one less year of life for me to experience. And that's scary when you think of it that way. It's the sand falling through the hourglass of your life. Less and less with each passing moment. But then I look at Bruce—and all that he's been through in the past year and especially the big challenge he faces now. And I remember thinking on Monday how great it was that despite all of that, he never stopped living life to the fullest. And maybe that's how I need to think. Not get concerned that the sand is running out but rather, be thankful that it's still falling."

J.P. Schmidt:

Good afternoon.

We leave our fingerprint on this world based on the life we lead and we all hope to leave a positive impact during our time here. We are here today to honor and celebrate the life of Bruce Hill, to talk about our memories of him and the impact he had on each of us, the fingerprints he left on our lives. I have thought a lot about what it is I want to share about Bruce this afternoon, the way he specifically impacted my life and the way I think about things.

They say there is beauty in simplicity. I'm a believer in this and I think Bruce more than anyone proved this to be true. Bruce didn't need fancy, expensive material things to find the joy in life, the joy in each day, the joy in each moment. Maybe this is why he stayed so positive throughout his illness, because he focused on the now, he relished in the moment at hand; he didn't rush or wish life away.

He enjoyed that moment he was in when he was caring for his lawn, or washing his vehicles, or going on a long walk with a loving dog. Bruce knew that each moment was a gift and he had a love for things that we often take for granted. I worked for years close to Bruce's childhood hometown, so we often discussed the area and when we did, boy did his face light up with delight. I would enjoy listening to the tales of his youth but more so enjoyed watching Bruce open up about it. Bruce didn't volunteer a lot of stories of his youth, nor did he discuss the future much, because again, he was more concerned with the now. If you asked him about certain memories or a specific time, he of course would share those stories with you. But usually it was Bruce asking about you, how are you? How's the family? How's my girl, Piper?

When you asked Bruce for help, he never hesitated, he simply said, "Okay." I remember the first time I brought Piper over to meet him. She was 12 weeks old and I think Bruce was 60. As she clumsily climbed up the stairs she was greeted by Bruce at the top of them. No, not standing there waiting for her. Bruce was instead down on the floor to greet her. He played with her, scratched her belly, let her climb all over him. I'm sure many of you have seen pictures of Bruce also down on the floor with his granddaughter, Ella. That's what Bruce did. He related to people, children, animals in the most simple but beautiful way. Whether a child or a puppy, he came down to their level. If he passed by a neighbor, he'd wave and say hello, cause in that moment, that's what you do. It's simple and it's beautiful.

I'll never forget the day Bruce was told his cancer was back. It was March 22, 2017. I remember this well because I was with Mrs. H. when she got the call from the doctor. The reason we were all together is because we were at the ICU in Dover as my Mom was in the final hours of her life. Mrs. H. told Bruce the news she received from the doctor, and in typical Bruce fashion, he simply nodded his head and said, "Okay," and immediately went back to focusing on my Mom. I wanted to share that because again I think it shows how much Bruce lived in the moment, even after receiving devastating news. He didn't look back, he didn't look ahead. He instead stayed with my family and focused on our needs in that difficult time. To Bruce, that was simple, to me it was beautiful.

Now on a lighter note, I wanted to share one of my favorite Bruce stories, which is when he was pulled over by the police. No, Bruce wasn't speeding. He didn't do anything illegal. He was pulled over because the police officer saw his pet sitting advertisement, told Bruce he needed a good pet sitter, and that he'd heard Bruce had a good reputation. I wasn't there but I am sure Bruce's response was probably, "Oh, okay."

I will miss talking sports with Bruce, watching how excited he got to discuss a great game or a great play. Now I am a Mets fan and any of you who might be as well known that's not an easy thing to be. But I am going to hold on to some hope here. I know the Yanks were Bruce's main baseball team. But in his final hours, the hospice nurse asked him what his favorite team was and yes, Bruce said, and I quote: "The Mets." So Bruce, with all the agony that comes with being a Mets fan, I'm going to forever hold on to the possibility that you entered Heaven rooting for the Mets.

Speaking of hospice, after Bruce had passed that night and Mrs. H., Chris, Doug, and I were leaving the hospital, the staff greeted us on our way down the hall. They offered their condolences and one of the nurses who had just come on duty told Mrs. H. she was sorry. Mrs. H. said to her, "I wish you could have known him. He was one of a kind." The nurse replied stating, "Oh, I knew him well." We all kind of looked at each other, thinking maybe this is standard hospice code. Act as if you knew the patient well? Mrs. H. said to her, "Oh, you did?" The nurse said, "Well yes, very well, he took care of my dogs for years." I don't know what it was, but it was exactly what we needed to hear in that moment of sadness. It was typical Bruce. We didn't think of the sadness we just experienced, or the sadness that would be coming in the near future. It gave us a laugh and a smile in that moment. It was simple and it was beautiful.

Bruce had said to me in the hospital that when he got out he wanted to have a party, a party at St. Jude's with family and friends. Bruce, we hope you enjoy your party. We thank you for leaving your fingerprints on our lives, for showing us the beauty in simplicity, for showing us the importance and beauty of living in the moment, for showing us how to appreciate the small things. Doug's eulogy mentioned three things Bruce always lived by: Be Good, Work Hard, Help Others. If I could add one more thing to that it would be to "Take time to smell the roses"—Bruce always did. So when you leave today and you think about Bruce, I encourage you to wave to your neighbors, get down on the floor with the children and pets in your lives, if someone asks for help and it's within your means, say, "Ok." And everyday, live in the moment—take time to smell the roses.

Now most of you know that Bruce was a phenomenal baseball player. If not for injury, he probably would have had a nice professional career playing it. In baseball, fans honor a great performance by giving a standing ovation known as a curtain call. So I am going to ask you all to stand, put your hands together and let's give Bruce and his life a well deserved curtain call!

Lisa Eidelberg:

Good afternoon. My name is Lisa and I am an almost 5-year pancreatic survivor and friend of Bruce and Linda's. I hope what I'm about to say doesn't come off as self-promoting because it is not the intention. When Linda told me the date of Bruce's Celebration of Life and asked me to speak, (For which I was so honored.) I knew I was on vacation that week. As we all love our coveted vacations, we all love Bruce more. There is not a shred of doubt that Bruce would have cut a vacation short and then some for a friend or family! Because Bruce was THAT person. If you asked him to help, he just simply did it—no questions. So how could I not follow his lead?!

I met Bruce and Linda two and a half years ago. It was a monthly PanCan meeting with our purple family when a new couple walked into the room. As is typical with these meetings, we went around the room and introduced ourselves (There are always new people.) and explained why we were there. When they got to Linda and Bruce, I remember thinking that Linda is incredibly supportive and such a kind soul even though she had dealt with her own tough times. Then we go to Bruce! Well, Bruce never met an audience or microphone he didn't like! He proceeded to talk and talk. He spoke confidently about his six-month survivorship, his Whipple, chemo, and how he will beat this monster. But in his first couple of sentences, what struck me immediately was his positive attitude, zest for life, and his determination. From that moment on, Bruce not only became a friend to all, but a passionate and active volunteer in raising awareness and funds for pancreatic cancer.

As Pietrina said, Bruce was always the first to volunteer for anything whether it was 10 degrees or 100 degrees. Bruce showed up with that big smile that would light up the room with a can-do attitude and a heart of gold. We volunteered many times together, be it Met Life, Overlook Hospital, or other events. For me personally, it was the Overlook lobby days that I enjoyed the most with Bruce as we had one on one conversations. It was those days that we had many discussions, whether it be about family (He did brag a lot about his family and rightfully so.), pancreatic cancer, dogs, or just life. One conversation really stood out to me. It was after Bruce's cancer came back and the struggles of chemo were slowing him down a bit (Remember, Bruce's "slowing down" was most others normal.). We talked about faith. He told me he truly believes that whatever happens is for a reason and it's God's plan. And he really believed that! My response to him was I'm so envious that you truly, deeply believe that, and I wish I could feel the same. This belief and faith helped him tremendously through tough times and in a way, I was envious of that belief. Bruce was also a dog lover and I'm afraid of dogs! As Gordon says, if dogs were allowed here today, Buddy would be sitting in the front row, wagging his tail! Human or animal, Bruce was good to all.

When Bruce was going through chemo, I sat with him one day as Linda was going through her own difficult times. Of course, being the good Jewish woman I am, I went with a bag of bagels, tuna, cream cheese, etc., some for Bruce and for the staff. Linda had told me he wasn't eating much. Ok, she was wrong. "Bruce, you want a bagel?" "SURE!" "Bruce, you want some tuna fish?" "Sure!" "Bruce, you want another bagel?" "Sure!" By the end of the few hours, the guy had eaten three maybe four bagels and all the tuna, leaving not much for the staff!

And in between, he was very busy telling all the other patients to be positive, relax, and just focus on surviving! And when the end was coming near, Bruce's will, determination, and ability to make others feel at ease never waned. As an almost 5-year pancreatic cancer survivor, I always thought I had a positive attitude. But next to Bruce, I felt like negative Nancy. His struggle serves all of us as a lesson to keep going no matter how difficult. Live life each and every day as if it's the last because you never know when it is. Bruce and I may have been different people outwardly, but our core and will to survive were as one.

Our purple family is struggling today with not only Bruce's loss, but other good, passionate volunteers, some battling as we speak. These angels are a constant reminder that we MUST continue to advocate and raise money so future generations never have to struggle with this heinous disease. These losses light fires in us to continue to find the cure!

Linda, I am humbled and honored to stand here today and speak about your incredible husband, Bruce. You are blessed with the memories of a man we can all learn from. Cherish those memories always and know, as survivors and warriors, Bruce's fight will not be in vain. The people here at Pancan and other organizations will not give up hope. A 9%-5 year survival rate is deplorable and we will continue to fight for Bruce, your beautiful family, and all others struggling with their own battle or loss!

The band, One Republic, has a song that has deep meaning to me. Some of the words are: "Hope that you spend your days and they all add up...I did it all. With every broken bone, I swear I lived!"

To Bruce...You sure did live!

We love you.

Mark Head:

Mohammed Ali once famously penned...

"Service to others is the rent we pay for our room here on this earth." By that standard Bruce paid his rent every single day of his life. He seemed drawn to doing the RIGHT things, for all the RIGHT reasons. Bruce was not flashy or ostentatious. He impressed me as the "strong, silent type," no bellyaching, no complaining, pure Forrest Gump. His service work was not done for the vain purpose of causing others to notice and laud his efforts, or so he could bask in the glory of his handy work. Bruce served others because this is who he was—period. Had it not been for his commitment to helping others besides himself, he and I may not have crossed paths. The same could be said of Linda as well. I first met Bruce and Linda, where else? At a Washington, D.C. gathering sponsored by the Pancreatic Cancer Action Network, also known as Pancreatic Cancer Advocacy Days.

Bruce and I were considered to be "long time survivors" at the time that we met last June. Far too few of our fellow pancreatic cancer patients live past the first year after diagnosis. We had converged there to lobby Congress to better support research and clinical trials so that we might improve the five year survival rate for Pancreatic Cancer. What is the five year survival rate for Pancreatic Cancer you might ask? An abysmal 9 percent are still alive post diagnosis. The ten year survival rate is a heartbreaking 1%. Pancreatic Cancer holds the distinction of being the only cancer type that has not made significant mortality improvement since 1971. Our hope for change is founded in the belief that the fruit of these labors will result, one day, in a CURE for this scourge that ravished too many.

At that meeting, Bruce and Linda and my wife, Donna, and I attended a dinner at a restaurant in The Capital District in Washington. That dinner was sponsored by the founder of NEGU, the Never Ever Give Up Facebook site for pancreatic cancer survivors and caregivers. Barry Reiter was supposed to be there with us, and like Bruce, Barry gave all of himself to his effort to stay alive and remain a person first, and a patient second. Barry was unable to be with us in D.C., and heartbreakingly, he died a few scant weeks before Bruce did.

At that first meeting, I was immediately struck by how down to earth and "real" the Hills were. I recognized Bruce's quiet energy that presented as "matter of fact"—"Oh yeah, I have Pancreatic Cancer but I will not let it get in the way of living my life." For PC survivors, that Stephen King "Shawshank Redemption" line, "Get busy living or get busy dying" holds special meaning. Bruce's penchant for living his life was by every lens through which one could examine such things, a cinematic testimonial of courage, positivity, and nobility. Bruce's humility was not feigned nor was it forced, it was authentic. Taxed with a death sentence of an illness, he refused to lay down or "boo hoo" on the pity pot, or to complain about it whatsoever. Bruce put cancer on a back burner up until the very end. It was never in the forefront unless it was about facing his chemo or undergoing a serious procedure, or about rallying others. Cancer had very little to do with Bruce's life plan for himself. It was near as I could tell an "inconvenience," something to live through, not something that defined him as a person. As a pancreatic cancer survivor myself, I marveled at his calm. When I found myself in his company, what I noticed the most was how calm I became when we were together, and that peacefulness remained with me after I parted his company.

Maya Angelou eloquently said once, "People will forget what you said. They may forget what you did, but they will never ever forget how you made them feel."

I imagine that Maya had people like Bruce in mind when she uttered those now famous words. Shortly after parting from his company that first time, my pulse rate dropped a few notches and my anxiety about the uncertainty of my own plight lessened. My own calm and peace became enhanced by his. His "chill" and unassuming nature became grafted to mine. This is what occurs when you are in the company of someone who commands a way of being that says, "Hey, You matter!!!" I am present here as much for you, as for myself. This scarcity of this "other-centered presence," laid bare for someone to grab a hold of is a rare commodity indeed. Laid back and unassuming, he accepted whatever life threw his way not from the petulant "Why me?" Perspective of many of us, but from the more rare and robust perspective of "What can I reasonably do about it now?" And then, "How can I carry myself in a way that will make Linda and the boys proud?" Folks, you just can't make this stuff up. I know that it is sometimes in vogue to "sanitize" a person after they pass in order for others to see them in a better light. A pardonable fib under indigent circumstances. An exercise in the American tradition of not letting the truth get in the way of a good story. An understandable purification ritual that is sometimes sorely needed to prop someone's image up.

For anyone who knew Bruce Hill, you know that in Bruce's chapter book of life this "clean up job" was never needed. It is not an exaggeration or a stretch of the truth for me to say that he was an extremely brave and genuinely "beautiful man." As Nelson Mandela once said, "I learned that courage is not an absence of fear but rather triumph over it. A brave man is not he who is unafraid, but he who conquers his fear." I know that Bruce is with us in spirit. He may actually be looking down and finding all the fuss totally unnecessary, and even in his present state of being, he may still find all of these chronicles a tad bit uncomfortable. Bruce was a simple man. Simple in all of the ways that matter in life. He stayed physically fit and didn't slow down. He loved his family, he loved nature and animals. The sound bites from his video blog for PC survivors were part "Rocky Balboa" and part "Mother Theresa." There are few people within someone's lifetime where we could legitimately proclaim, "It has been my great honor and privilege to have met them." For the record, Bruce is on that short list for me. Bruce falls into that rare category of person that you were proud to have met because the entire time that you were in their presence, they made you feel better for having been placed in their orbits around the sun.

Deep in the recesses of all our souls, there is a voice that cries out when you meet that "special someone" whose essence is pure goodness, kindness, and love. That is who Bruce was. As we come together in this community of love to celebrate this extraordinary man, I know one thing for certain. In this sometimes cruel and too often random world, anyone who had the good fortune to come in contact with this very good man was better off as a result of it. His footprint was a quiet, albeit a very certain and pure one. Aside from loving his family in a thorough and complete way, Bruce's love and service to others had to have been his crowning achievement. His sublime understanding that a life well lived was best defined through actions, not words, through humility, not boastfulness, and through courage, not fret and worry, are the very hallmarks by which I shall always remember him.

Bruce, my friend, my fellow traveler on this scary and uncertain road, it has been my absolute pleasure to have made your acquaintance. You never failed to remind me of all that is good that is contained within my fellow man.

I spoke with Linda a few short days before Bruce passed on. She informed me that Bruce wanted to be certain that he was "dying the right way." He wanted to be sure that his passing was not causing a burden for Linda and the boys. Marvelous resolve, he truly had a divine presence within him, to be so close to the end of his life here, and yet still have the presence of mind and the clarity of heart to be more concerned for others than for himself. The only bit of justice in Bruce's being taken "too soon," is that the vibrancy of his spirit survives. It has taken residence in all of us here and within many others. Rest easy, Bruce, you did it right. Linda and the boys will be just fine.

You died as you lived, humbly, and more concerned for others than for yourself. Just as importantly you never, ever, ever gave up. No one who gives it their all could ever be said to have "lost their battle with cancer." Bruce didn't lose his battle, he simply ran out of time.

In closing and in the spirit of celebrating his life, I would like to conclude this testimonial with the words of Henry Scott Holland:

Death is nothing at all
I have only slipped away into the next room.
I am I and you are you. Whatever we were to each other,
That, we still are.
Call me by my old familiar name.
Speak to me in the easy way
Which you always used.
Put no difference into your tone.
Wear no forced air of solemnity or sorrow.
Laugh as we always laughed
At the jokes we enjoyed together.
Play, smile, think of me. Pray for me.
Let my name be ever the household word that it always was.
Let it be spoken without effect.
Without the trace of a shadow on it.
Life means all that it ever meant.
It is the same that it ever was.
There is absolute unbroken continuity.
Why should I be out of mind
Because I am out of sight?
I am but waiting for you.
For an interval somewhere very near.
Just around the corner.
All is well. Nothing is past; nothing is lost. One brief moment and all will
be as it was before, only better—Infinitely happier and forever we will all
be one together with Christ.
(By Henry Scott Holland)

May Bruce's peace that resides in the peace of Christ be with you.

Speech Given in Honor of Bruce at New Jersey Purple Stride

11/10/19
By Lisa Eidelberg

BE GOOD, WORK HARD, HELP OTHERS. Words that our friend and fellow volunteer, Bruce Hill, lived by. Bruce, a 3-year pancreatic cancer survivor, sadly lost his battle with the monster in January. We met Bruce and his wife, Linda, at his first PanCan meeting where we introduce ourselves and explain why we are volunteering. According to Linda, Bruce was somewhat quiet before his diagnosis. He found his voice through cancer and came out of his shell. And boy he sure did!! He proceeded to talk and talk. He spoke about his six-month survivorship and how he will beat this monster. What struck me immediately was his positive attitude, zest for life, and his determination.

From that moment on, Bruce not only became a friend to all, but a passionate and active volunteer in raising awareness and funds for pancreatic cancer. Bruce was always the first to volunteer, showing up with a smile that would light up the room, a can-do attitude, and a heart of gold.

We volunteered many times together but it was the Overlook Hospital lobby days where we had many conversations. But one really stood out to me. It was after Bruce's cancer came back and the struggles of chemo were slowing him down. We talked about faith. He told me he truly believes that whatever happens is for a reason and it's God's plan. And he really believed that! That belief and faith helped him tremendously through tough times and in a way, I was envious of that belief.

I accompanied Bruce to chemo one day as Linda was going through her own difficult times. As he downed four bagels and a container of tuna, Bruce was busy telling the other patients to be positive, relax, and to just focus on surviving! And when the end was coming near, Bruce's ability to make others feel at ease never waned. One of his last words to me were when he was in Hackensack Hospital, struggling. He turned to me and said, "I worry about Linda...I just want her to be okay. I will be fine." To the end, his main concern was everyone else!

His struggle teaches us a lesson to live life each day as if it's the last because you don't know when it is.

Our Purple Family is struggling this year with not only Bruce's loss, but Franco's as well. These angels, and many others, are a constant reminder that we MUST continue to advocate and raise money so future generations don't struggle with this heinous disease. These losses light fires in us!

As a five and a half year pancreatic cancer survivor, I will not let Bruce's journey be in vain. The people here at Pancan and other organizations will not give up hope. A 9%-5 year survival rate is deplorable and we will continue to fight for Bruce, (Otherwise known as "Papa Broosh" to his precious granddaughter, Ella.) his family, and all others struggling their own battle or loss.

So to Bruce, we will continue to **BE GOOD, WORK HARD AND HELP OTHERS IN YOUR MEMORY!**

WE MISS YOU!

Testimonials

Since Bruce was first diagnosed with pancreatic cancer and continuing through the present day, I have received hundreds of beautiful messages from family and friends. What follows are a handful of those messages. (For privacy purposes, I have omitted all names except for family members.)

Shortly before midnight on Thursday night, January 17th, Bruce's fight came to an end. After a rapid decline the past few weeks, he knew it was time. As he left the hospital to head for hospice, in typical Bruce fashion, he thanked all of the nurses who cared for him. Then he told them, "It's time for me to go."—Chris Palermo, Bruce's stepson

I'm so sorry to hear about Bruce's passing. I will always remember his smiling face and his fierce dedication to getting better and fighting the disease. You both were such amazing advocates who helped so many people through your blog and attendance at so many events.

I have met a lot of people in my life, but only a few are like Bruce: Those who truly don't have a negative or bad thought in their body. They exude unwavering goodness!

Bruce and Linda were the first couple to greet me at my first Pancreatic Cancer Advocacy Days in Washington, D.C. Bruce was passionate about raising hope and helping others to fight this terrible disease. I will never forget Bruce.

Bruce was a hero to all who faced catastrophic conditions. He was a beacon of hope for all.

The world has lost a wonderful man who fought the beast of pancreatic cancer for three years. He was such an inspiration to everyone he met, along with his sweet wife, Linda, who is fighting renal cancer. He spent the last three years advocating for research and helping newly diagnosed patients. He was extremely friendly and warm. You couldn't help but become friends with him and Linda immediately upon meeting them.

Thursday night my family lost one of their strongest fighters. Bruce not only made a huge impact on the Pancreatic Cancer Community, but his positive attitude made an impact on our family as well. He will always be an inspiration to me. Because of him I know I can do anything I put my mind to. Rest easy, Bruce. You will be greatly missed.—Gianna Sacco-Calderone, daughter of Linda's cousin

My strongest memories of Bruce are fittingly from the Stomp. Back in 2016, a few months after his surgery, I had the honor of walking with Bruce during the 5K. By the end of it you could forget what he had gone through. It was the same Bruce I had always known. Not many people can battle such a terrible disease and maintain such an extremely positive attitude. But not many people are Bruce. The next year, at the Stomp, I learned that Bruce's cancer had returned. No complaints, no woe is me, he would keep on fighting it because that's who he was. Bruce did win out in what he did, in what he showed people as he courageously fought and never wavered. I can't think of anyone nicer than Bruce. He was a truly great man!

It has been my honor and privilege to get to know Bruce and call him friend. In the face of pancreatic cancer and all that means, he inspired hope and positivity with every breath he took. I will miss him terribly. My heart goes out to you, Linda, on this profound loss.

Bruce was one of those people who taught how to be through his actions. He will live on in spirit, as he inspired so many people to live in the best way possible.

You and your family and friends have been blessed in sharing precious years with "a man among men." I am so sorry that you and his extended world are no longer going to benefit from his joy of life and love for living. Please accept my heartfelt sympathies at your personal loss—and all that Bruce gifted to the world. A very kind and caring man who will be missed by so many. What a privilege to have had his love.

Even in the face of pancreatic cancer, Bruce gave the world 110% of his kindness and generosity. He was kind, gracious, and an inspiration to all who knew him. He won his fight with cancer with integrity and fortitude. He was a man who didn't let his cancer stop him from living life—active, energetic, and positive. On a day like today (in NJ), it's windy and pouring rain. Bruce would say, "It's a beautiful day." We can all learn a lesson in life from Bruce. Count your blessings, life is short. Bruce never stopped smiling. He was a light in everyone's life.

On Thursday, my hero, Bruce Hill, passed away. What made Bruce my hero was that he showed me that you could have cancer and still live your life. That sounds like a simple thing, but it really isn't. The cultural messages we get about cancer tend to be either: 1) Your life is over; or 2) You are now a warrior, a survivor, a superhero—something fundamentally different from the person you used to be. Don't get me wrong. I love being #SuperLaura, but what I really needed to know when I was diagnosed was that I could go to chemo and still keep picking up my son from school. I needed to know that I could have cancer and still be me. And that was what I learned from Bruce. Looking at Bruce as he went to the gym, mowed the lawn, and shoveled snow, you would never have known he was "sick." 2018 was Bruce's third year of pancreatic cancer, and he still drove Linda down to DC three times that year to help me take care of my family, and advocate for pancreatic cancer research that will help people he'd never even meet. Because that's just what Bruce did. That was just Bruce being himself. When I got cancer, I thought, I want to be like Bruce. I am so grateful to have known him so that he could be my role model through this. Thank you, Bruce.—Laura Wells, Bruce's daughter-in-law and cancer survivor and warrior

We nurses can not believe Bruce is gone. He was the true definition of a fighter. His three sayings: Be Good, Work Hard, Help Others: Bruce truly did live his life that way. I was in awe of his fighting spirit and how he wasn't going down without a fight. He was so kind to other patients and very caring. I loved talking about going to the gym with him because it inspired me to hear that he went! I think of him when I go to the gym and smile. Bruce made such an impact on many people and blessed people with his presence. I'm so glad I got to know him. I realize that people are placed in our lives for many different reasons. I'm glad you both got placed in mine. Bruce will always have a place in my heart and I will always smile when I think of him.

I was lucky to have met Bruce. He did a blog. He made speeches. He tried things outside of his comfort zone. Perhaps the greatest lesson that

Bruce taught me is that as long as you are yourself you can do anything. He did those things with the spirit of wanting to help others and to make a difference. God only knows who may have seen his blog, heard his story, or heard him speak and were changed. He had the courage to help others even if he couldn't help himself. That's what Heroes do. Heroes think of others. Heroes know how to be themselves. Heroes are not afraid to try things outside of their comfort zone. Thank you so much, Bruce, for this life lesson. Thank you, Bruce, for being my friend.

Late Thursday night our village lost one of the strongest and most positive men one would ever know. Bruce was the husband of my first grade teacher, Linda Hill. He was diagnosed with pancreatic cancer about three years ago.To most, this diagnosis would ruin them, but not Bruce. It made him stronger and more determined to spread the importance of positive thinking. He never gave up, he spread the word and raised awareness of not only his horrible disease but also Dylan's. He would tell Dylan's story whenever he could and referred to Dylan as his "hero." He attended events for Dylan and completed the Stomp several times, even a few days after receiving treatment. As I looked through pictures of the two of them, I was amazed that despite their age difference they both have impacted the world greatly and together beat the odds of two horrible diseases. I am not only lucky to own one of these heroes, but to have known another real life hero for so many years. The road ahead won't be easy for so many but Bruce taught us all so much and we will continue to be inspired by him throughout our lives. In the end one can only hope to leave behind a legacy as amazing and inspiring as Bruce Hill. I told Dylan yesterday morning that he has the strongest angel watching over him now and I have no doubt he will be there for Dylan and us always. Please keep his family, especially his amazing wife, in your thoughts and prayers as they navigate the very difficult time ahead.

We said goodbye to Bruce today—couldn't have been a more perfect tribute. After the busy day, as we were getting Ella ready for bed tonight, she points to my phone and says to me, "Call Papa Bruce?" I choked up a bit and told her we can't call Papa Bruce anymore. Without missing a beat she replies with her second choice, "Call Santa?" When you rank above Santa in the eyes of a child, that says something. But that was Bruce.— Chris Palermo, Bruce's stepson

PART SEVEN

Caregiving and Grief

Caregiving:

In successive years, Bruce and I became each other's caregivers. When you're both dealing with cancer, "In sickness and in health" takes on new meaning. No more taking each other's health for granted. No more taking each other for granted. Your total focus is on caring for your partner and hopefully nursing him or her back to health. You don't think about yourself or your own needs. It's all about your loved one. If the illness is prolonged, it can take its toll not only on the patient but on the caregiver as well. You become a nurse, nutritionist, researcher, organizer of all things medical, primary caller of doctors, nurses, and family who need to be informed, and spiritual counselor to your partner as he or she navigates the most difficult physical and emotional time of their lives. As a daily caregiver for three years, I can attest that it's an indefatigable job. What helped keep me afloat was the support of family and friends, working out, praying, meditating, and continuing to live as "normal" a life as possible—with lots of love, laughter, and joy. If you are a caregiver, don't neglect your own needs (Yes, I realize how hard that is.). It's not being selfish to take care of yourself—it's necessary for your own survival as well as your partner's. Take each day, each treatment, and each surgery as they come, with optimism, hope, and faith. As Bruce said every time he had a setback: "This is just a bump in the road."

Grief:

I am a retired educator with no background in grief counseling. My views on the grieving process come strictly from my own experience.

Grief is inevitable after losing a loved one. I don't think you can heal until you go through the grieving process. The first year was particularly hard for me. Bruce wasn't here for all of the holidays. He wasn't here for our birthdays. He wasn't here for family barbecues in the summer. Bruce was a "people person" and enjoyed all of our family and friends' gatherings. His absence created a deep, silent void. And the grief would hit me hardest at those times. I missed his empty chair at the kitchen table. I missed not seeing him out on our sun porch sitting in his recliner watching sports on t.v. I missed watching him work on our lawn. I missed seeing him interacting with our grandchildren. I missed seeing him play with beloved dogs. I missed going places with him, even if it was just a car ride. I missed his company. I missed his friendship and love. I missed talking with him about absolutely anything. I just missed him.

I found my grief came in waves and often at unexpected times. I mostly saved my tears for private times. I knew my family and friends loved and supported me, but I also knew how uncomfortable it would be for me and them to show my feelings publicly. I believe it's hard for most people who can't relate to your loss to find the right words to say. People often caringly ask, "How are you doing?" I knew in my heart that they wanted to hear that I was fine. Few people can handle the intense emotions of a person in the throes of grief. Small talk becomes the norm and it's really okay. It can actually be a welcome distraction. At least it was for me.

My parents were married for 60 years when my father passed away. My mother was a widow from the age of 80 to the age of 90, when she too passed. Throughout those ten years, she lived alone and she lived independently. She continued to live her life and continued to enjoy her family and friends, and volunteering at her church. So she became my role model without even knowing it. My mantra became: "If mom could do this, then so can I."

Just as helping other cancer survivors helped Bruce and me cope with our own health issues, helping others who are grieving brings me comfort, hope, and satisfaction. I belong to two cancer sites. I began reaching out to widows and widowers and offering them the benefit of sharing a grief that I sadly understood. Mostly we communicate on-line but occasionally, we talk over the phone. I know their pain and they know mine. There's no pretense between us. There are no barriers to climb over. We may be long distance friends but our bonds run deep and are strong. I am grateful for each one of them.

After I retired, I volunteered in our school district. But when Bruce became sick, I had to give that up to devote my time to him. After he passed and I felt ready to do so, I resumed volunteering in school. Volunteering, being back in the classroom, and being with children gave my life purpose and brought me fulfillment and joy.

Other things that helped me were maintaining normalcy as much as possible. I continued to work-out, visit family, and keep to a regular routine. I also joined a local support group for a time. Talking with others in a safe place can be beneficial. So can offering advice, support, and friendship to other group members. You may benefit from a support group or you may benefit more from a walk in the woods. Or, you may find that you need professional help. We are all different and we all grieve differently. Do what's best for you. But do something everyday. Cry when you feel the need to but don't forget to laugh! Let yourself feel joy. Your loss will always be with you. But so will the beautiful memories of your loved ones. Here's to your memories and here's to my own memories of thirty years with Bruce A. Hill!

Afterword

By Pamela Acosta Marquardt,
Founder, Pancreatic Cancer Action Network

I will never forget standing in the hospital room while the doctor shared the news with my mother that she had a tumor on her pancreas and that it was cancer. When I said, "Okay, so what is the next step?", he simply looked down at his shoes.

My first thought was, "Oh my gosh, that is the disease that Michael Landon had!" And I recalled that he had lost his battle rather quickly. My next thought was, "I'll go on the new "World WideWeb" and find the organization that focuses on pancreatic cancer so that I can save my mother's life!" I was mortified when my search netted no results—there was not a single organization anywhere in the world focusing on pancreatic cancer.

The only place I found any information was in an online discussion board dedicated to pancreatic cancer hosted by Ralph Hruban, MD, a pathologist at Johns Hopkins University Medical Center. I was shocked that there were only a handful of participants. That discussion group became my lifeline as I sought out answers in an effort to save my mother. But as time went on, what I found was that more and more people kept coming to this group because there was nowhere else to turn. I found myself being there for others as much as I was there for myself. I knew then that something had to be done.

Being the compliant patient that she was, my mother followed doctor's orders and died in six months, just as they had prescribed.

By December of 1997, a year had passed and I noticed that those seeking support on the discussion board were becoming increasingly frustrated by the lack of resources for the pancreatic cancer community. There were simply no organizations solely dedicated to assisting those affected by the disease or anyone advocating on their behalf.

During the time that my mother battled pancreatic cancer, I discovered that quite a large number of celebrities and notable figures had lost their lives to pancreatic cancer—not just Michael Landon, but Donna Reed, Juliet Prowse, Henry Mancini, Paul Mitchell, Fernando Lamas, John Beradino, Fred Gwynne, Dizzy Gillespie and more. And since those early days, we have lost people like Luciano Pavoratti, Patrick Swayze, Steve Jobs, Sally Ride and many others. I had watched what had happened with the AIDS movement—no one wanted to talk about AIDS until celebrities stepped out to tout the importance of finding the answers.

I found out that there was a doctor at Johns Hopkins who wanted to study early detection for pancreatic cancer but there was no funding to establish his lab. It was at that moment that my grief collided with my creativity and the movement began.

I decided to produce a black-tie celebrity gala in Beverly Hills, California, to raise money to fund the development of the early detection research lab for Michael Goggins, MD, associate professor of Pathology and Oncology at the Sol Goldman Pancreatic Cancer Research Center at the Johns Hopkins University School of Medicine. I pitched the idea to my newfound friends in the discussion group and many of them became excited about the idea and agreed to help. Now I just had to rally those in the celebrity community who had a reason to care about pancreatic cancer!

After noticing that Michael Landon, Jr. had a letter posted on the Johns Hopkins website, I was able to connect with him. His father, the actor, had passed away from pancreatic cancer in 1991 at age 54. As I began to get connected to members of other celebrity families who had been affected by pancreatic cancer, scores of additional high-profile individuals became involved. The fundraiser gala, "An Evening with the Stars," took place on November 18, 1998, and was an extraordinary success, raising more than $165,000 to fund the establishment of Dr.Goggins' lab.

Attendees at the first fundraiser included many well-known celebrities whose loved ones had been touched by pancreatic cancer, including the family of Michael Landon; the family and company employees of Paul Mitchell; Esther Williams, the widow of Fernando Lamas; B.J. Allen, the companion of Juliet Prowse; fashionista Mr. Blackwell; E.J. Peaker, who lost her mother to the disease; Pat Boone; Connie Stevens; Stella Stevens; Anna Marie Horsford; the family of Henry Mancini; Mary Owen, the daughter of Donna Reed; Majorie Beradino, the wife of actor John Beradino from "General Hospital"; Dick Van Patten; singer Freda Payne; and many more.

As the organization took shape in the months that followed, help came from across the country. A New York attorney who'd lost both of his parents to pancreatic cancer contacted me and offered to help by establishing a 501(c)(3) corporation for the new charity, pro bono. Another supporter volunteered to create a website.

Sheila Kaplan, a former CNBC reporter based in Washington, D.C., provided assistance that proved to be especially valuable—she had lost her mother to pancreatic cancer and she put me in touch with Terry Lierman, the owner of Capitol Associates, one of the largest healthcare lobbying firms on Capitol Hill. Terry, who had lost his father to pancreatic cancer, lent his considerable political expertise to guide me in how our advocacy efforts should be shaped. At our first meeting, we decided upon the new organization's name: the Pancreatic Cancer Action Network, or PanCAN. He stressed the importance of every single word in the name.

In February of 1999, after months of hard work, the Pancreatic Cancer Action Network was officially incorporated and formally launched. From the start, hundreds of volunteers were at the ready to build awareness for the long-misunderstood and neglected disease. In 2000, we hired our first full time employee, Julie Fleshman, as Executive Director. In 2004, she was appointed President and CEO and has been at the helm ever since, leading the organization in bold and fearless innovation as we continue to push to get pancreatic cancer across the finish line sooner, rather than later.

The contributions of so many people, whether through time spent volunteering, making a donation, or both, have helped us advance research, support patients and create hope for those facing pancreatic cancer. This incredible support has enabled us to grow from a small startup to where we are today—the leading force in the fight against pancreatic cancer.

Pamela Acosta Marquardt
Founder,
Pancreatic Cancer Action Network, www.pancan.org

For My Husband

(Author unknown)

You filled the world with special joy and happiness untold
You always had a sunny way and a lovely heart of gold
You made life so much brighter just by being thoughtful, too,
And saying kind and helpful things was typical of you.
That's why it's hard to face the world and know you won't be there,
Lighting up life so warmly with your smile beyond compare.
The memories you left behind grow sweeter day by day
But you are missed, dear loved one, more
than any words can ever say.

CPSIA information can be obtained
at www.ICGtesting.com
Printed in the USA
LVHW042236300720
662016LV00002B/361